American Song Collection for

# Clarinet and Piano

James Marshall

Piano Accompaniment

The Cecilio CT-480 clarinet image on the cover is courtesy of Cecilio Musical Instruments.

© 2021 by Mel Bay Publications, Inc. All Rights Reserved.

WWW.MELBAY.COM

# *Preface*

***American Song Collection for Clarinet and Piano*** is a set of ten songs primarily derived from the Colonial to Civil War eras. Moderate in difficulty for the clarinet with D above the staff as the highest note, these songs find a unique expression in the hauntingly lyrical tone of the instrument. The wide ranges of both the piano and clarinet offer further textural pairings and contrasts within a traditional chordal harmonic framework with colorations of fourths, fifths, and occasional added tones. The collection consists of ballads, traditional and sacred songs including tunes from the "Sacred Harp" shape-note tradition. The most adventurous and colorful arrangement, "Black Is the Color of My True Love's Hair" shows more recent influences of Gershwin, Debussy, and Southern jazz.

"Prospect", the final song from the "Sacred Harp", includes the lyric:

*Oh if my Lord would come to meet*
*my soul would strength her wings in haste*
*Fly fearless through Death's iron gate*
*Nor feel the terrors as she passed.*

My thanks to William Bay for his guidance and advice in the creation of this collection.

**Song Listing:**

*Morning Song* – "Sacred Harp"
*Amazing Grace* – Music from "Virginia Harmony", Lyrics by John Newton
*Hard Times, Come Again* – Stephen Foster
*Camptown Races* – Reel – Stephen Foster
*Anthem* – "Sacred Harp"
*Black Is the Color of My True Love's Hair* – Southern Appalachian Folk Song
*Aura Lee* – Civil War Song
*Poor Wayfaring Stranger* – American Folk Song
*Yorktown* – Colonial Fife and Drum Song
*Prospect* – "Sacred Harp"

*James Marshall*

# *Index of Solos*

# *Morning Song*

Kentucky Harmony
Arr. James Marshall

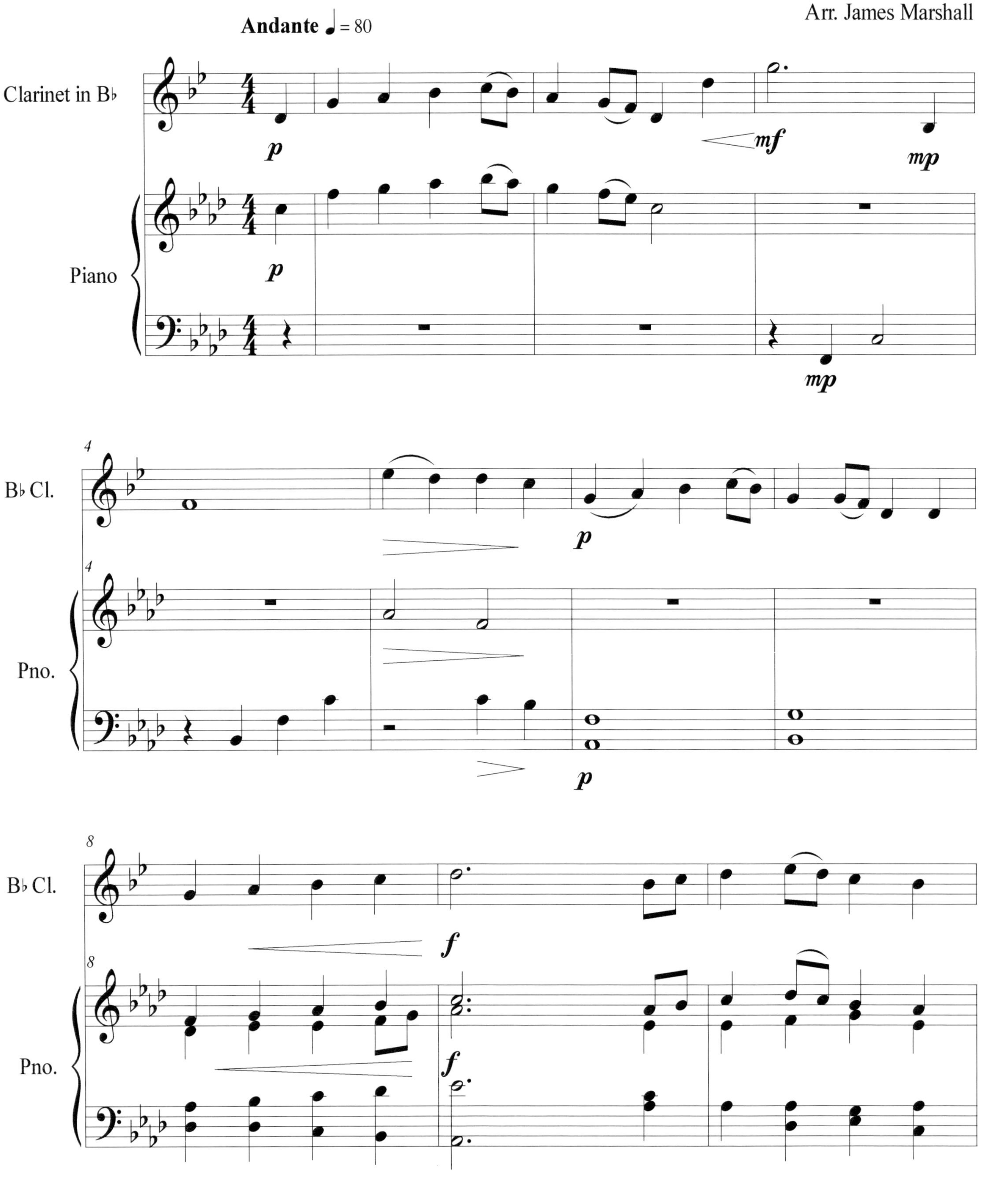

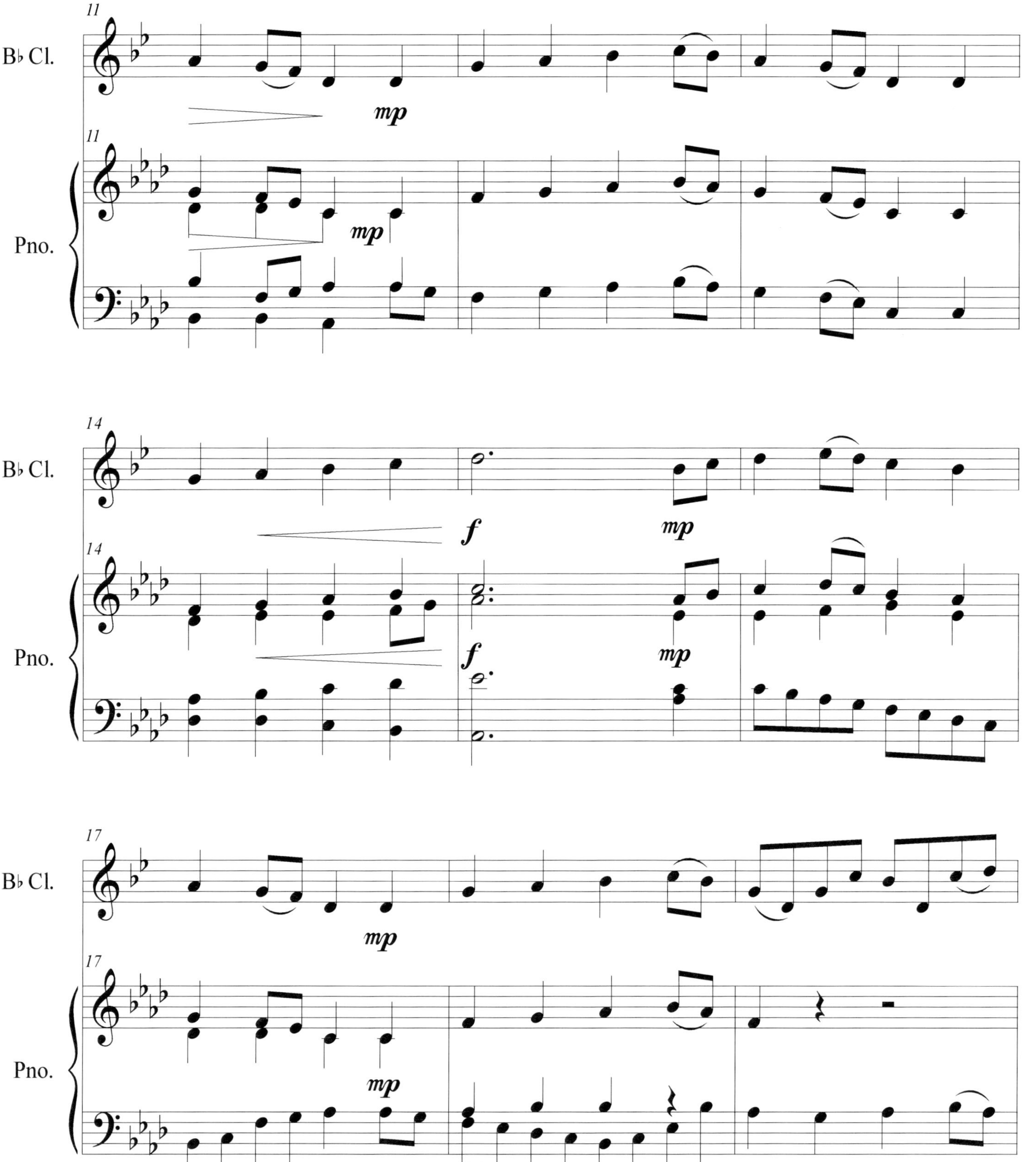
11
B♭ Cl.
mp
Pno.
mp
14
B♭ Cl.
f
mp
Pno.
f
mp
17
B♭ Cl.
mp
Pno.
mp

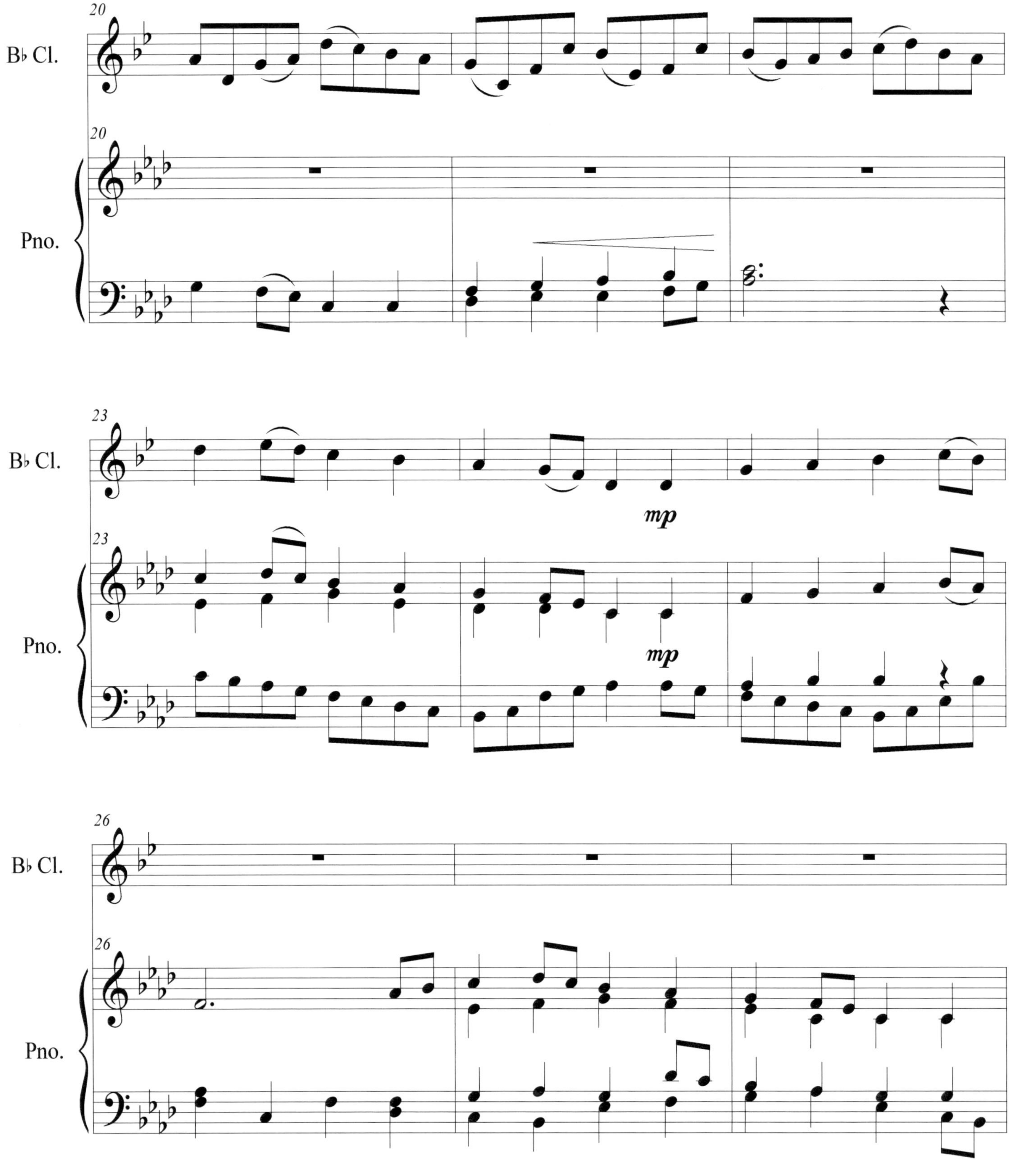
20
B♭ Cl.
20
Pno.
23
B♭ Cl.
mp
23
Pno.
mp
26
B♭ Cl.
26
Pno.

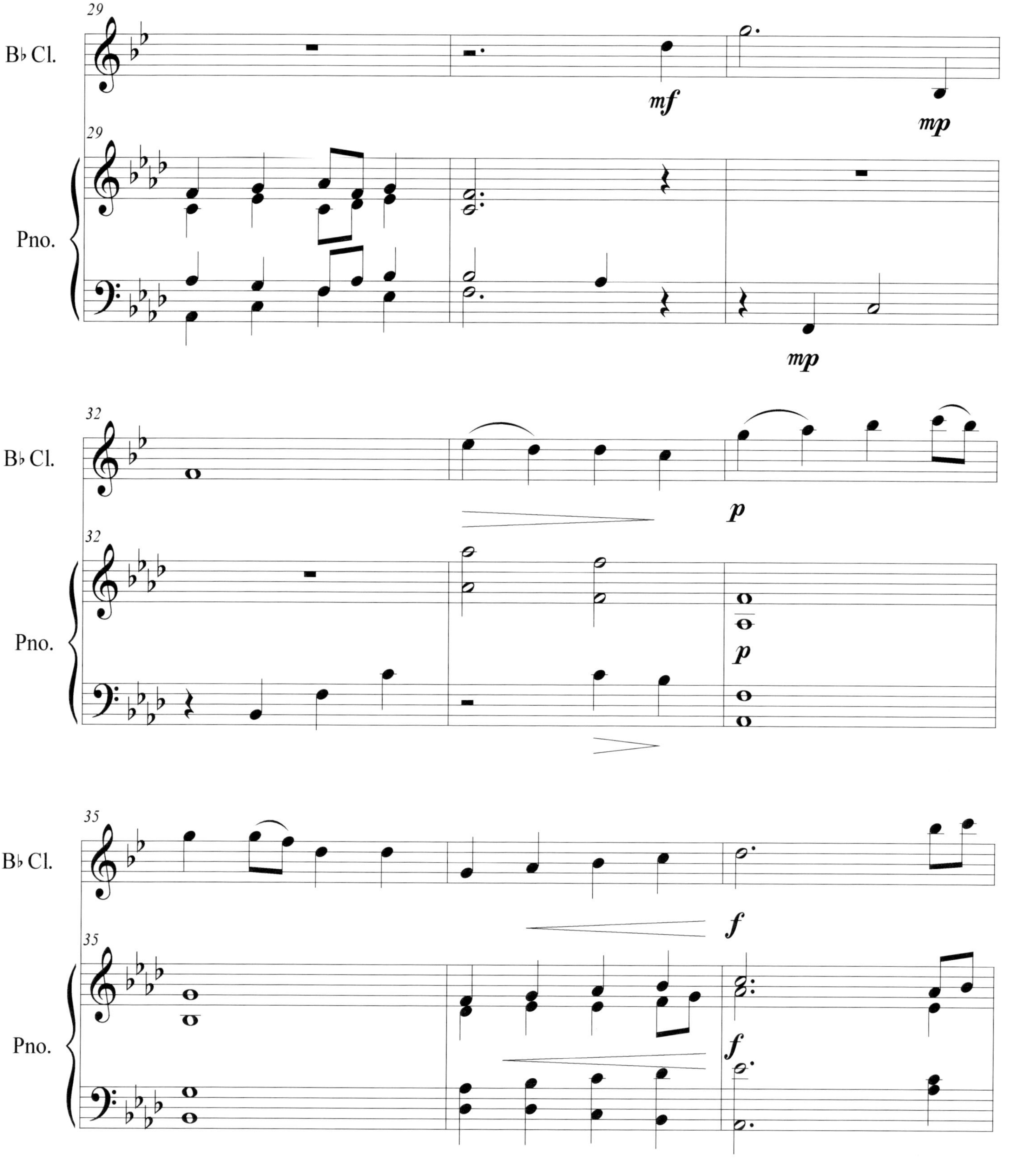
29
B♭ Cl.
Pno.
mf
mp
mp
32
p
p
35
f
f

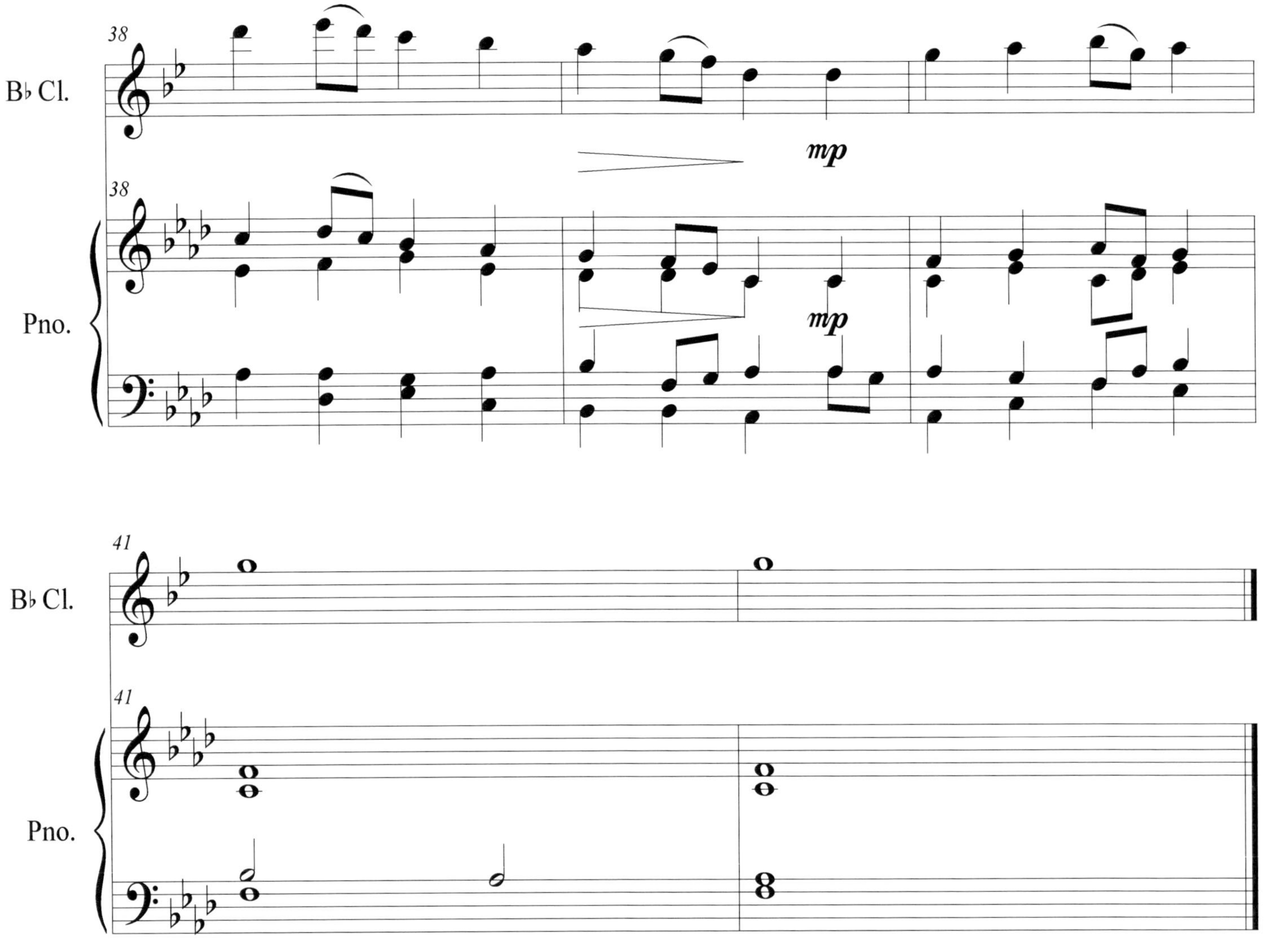
38
B♭ Cl.
mp
38
Pno.
mp
41
B♭ Cl.
41
Pno.

# *Amazing Grace*

Early American Melody

Arr. James Marshall

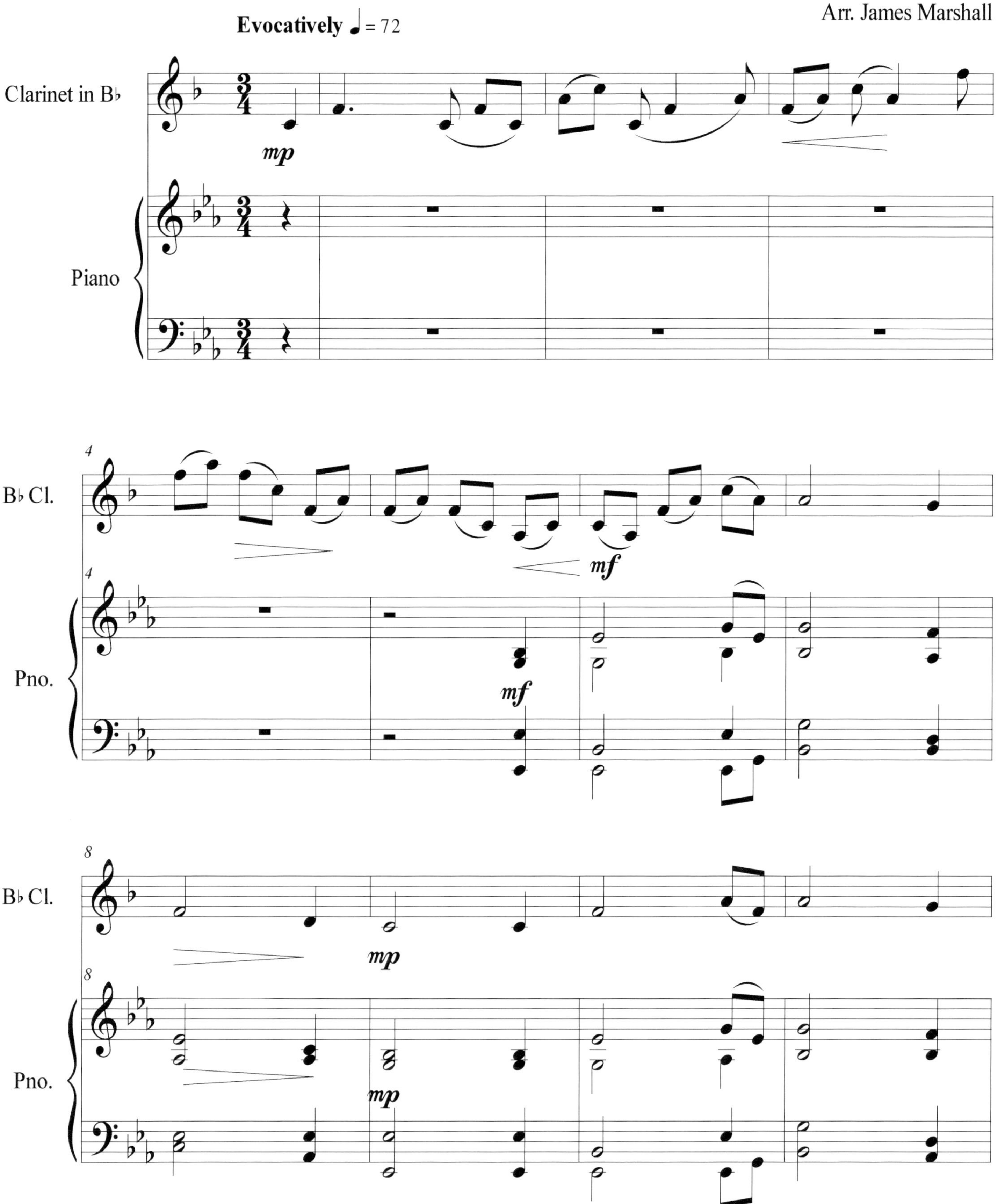

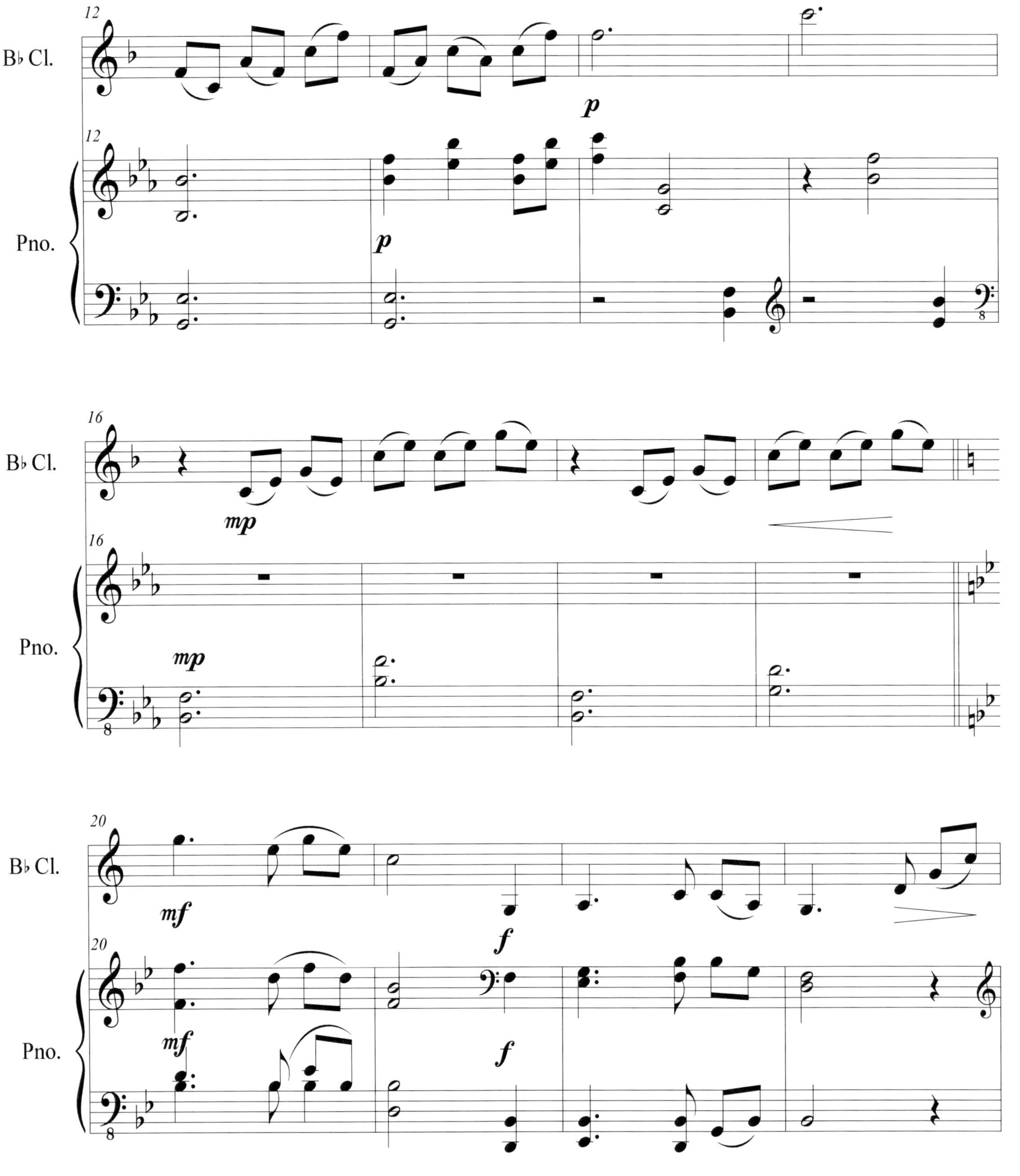
12
B♭ Cl.
Pno.
p
p
16
B♭ Cl.
Pno.
mp
mp
20
B♭ Cl.
Pno.
mf
f
mf
f

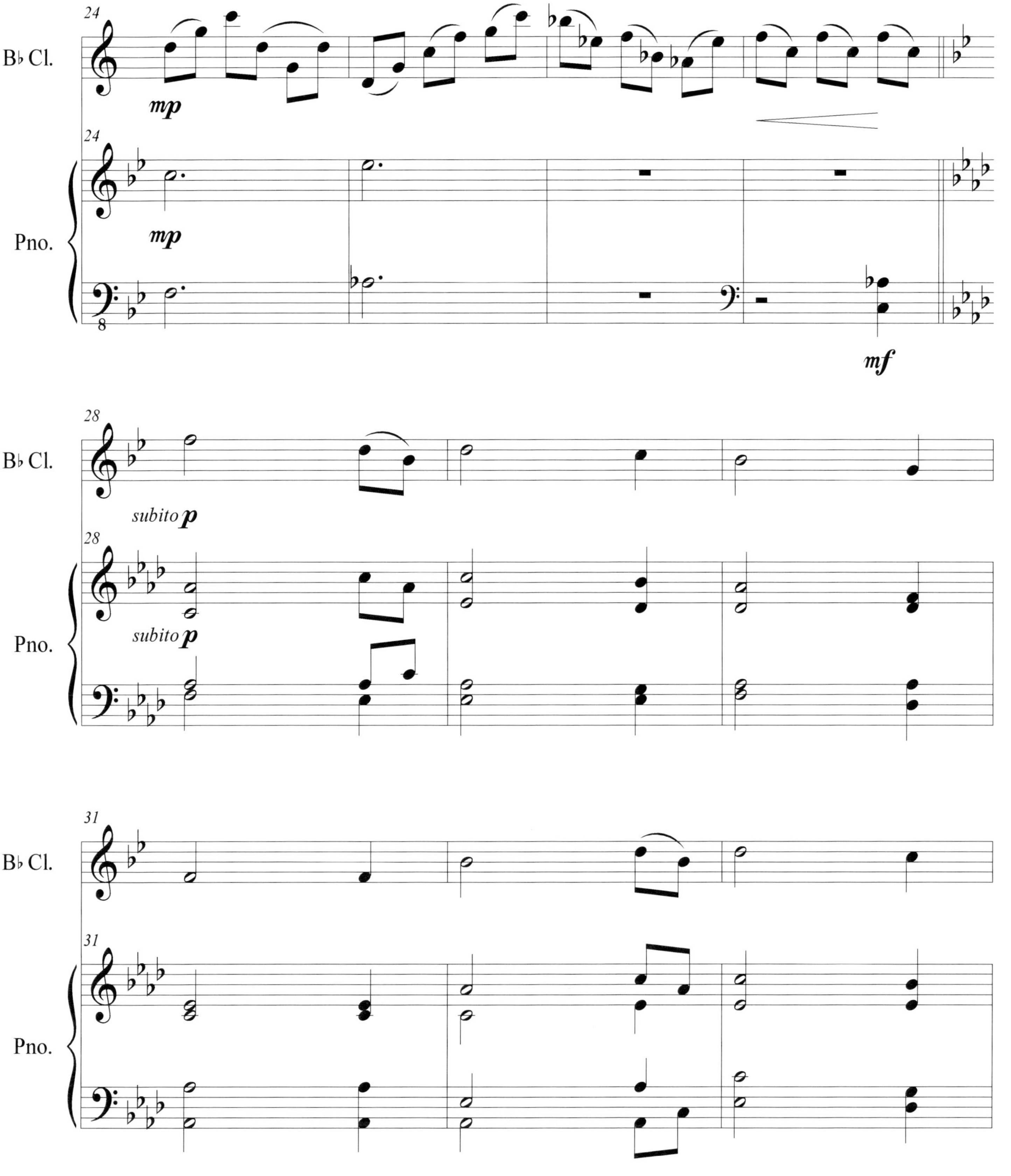
B♭ Cl.
Pno.
mp
mf
subito p

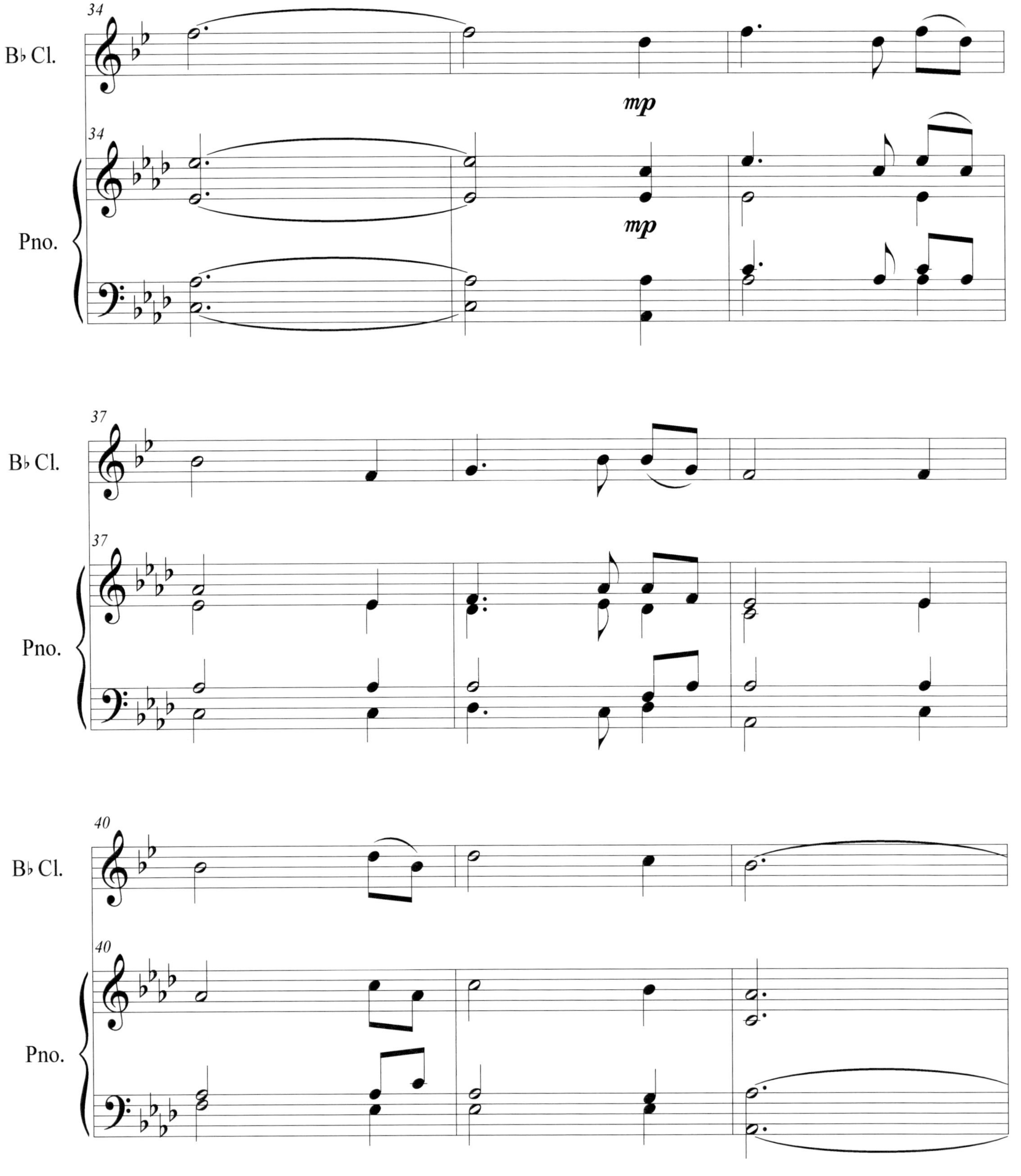

34
B♭ Cl.
mp
34
mp
Pno.
37
B♭ Cl.
37
Pno.
40
B♭ Cl.
40
Pno.

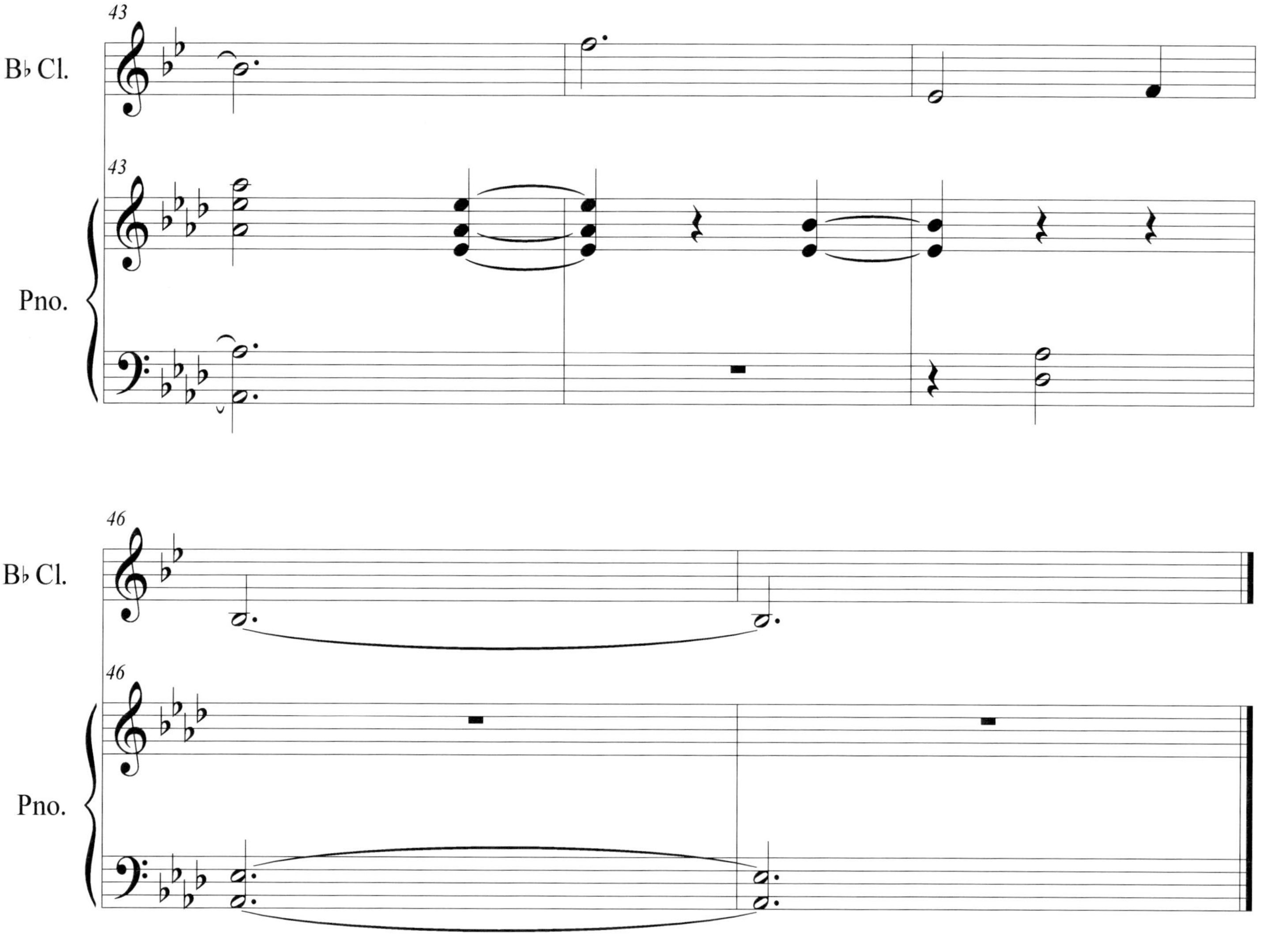
43
B♭ Cl.
43
Pno.
46
B♭ Cl.
46
Pno.

# *Hard Times, Come Again No More*

Stephen Foster

Arr. James Marshall

**Reminiscing** ♩ = 66

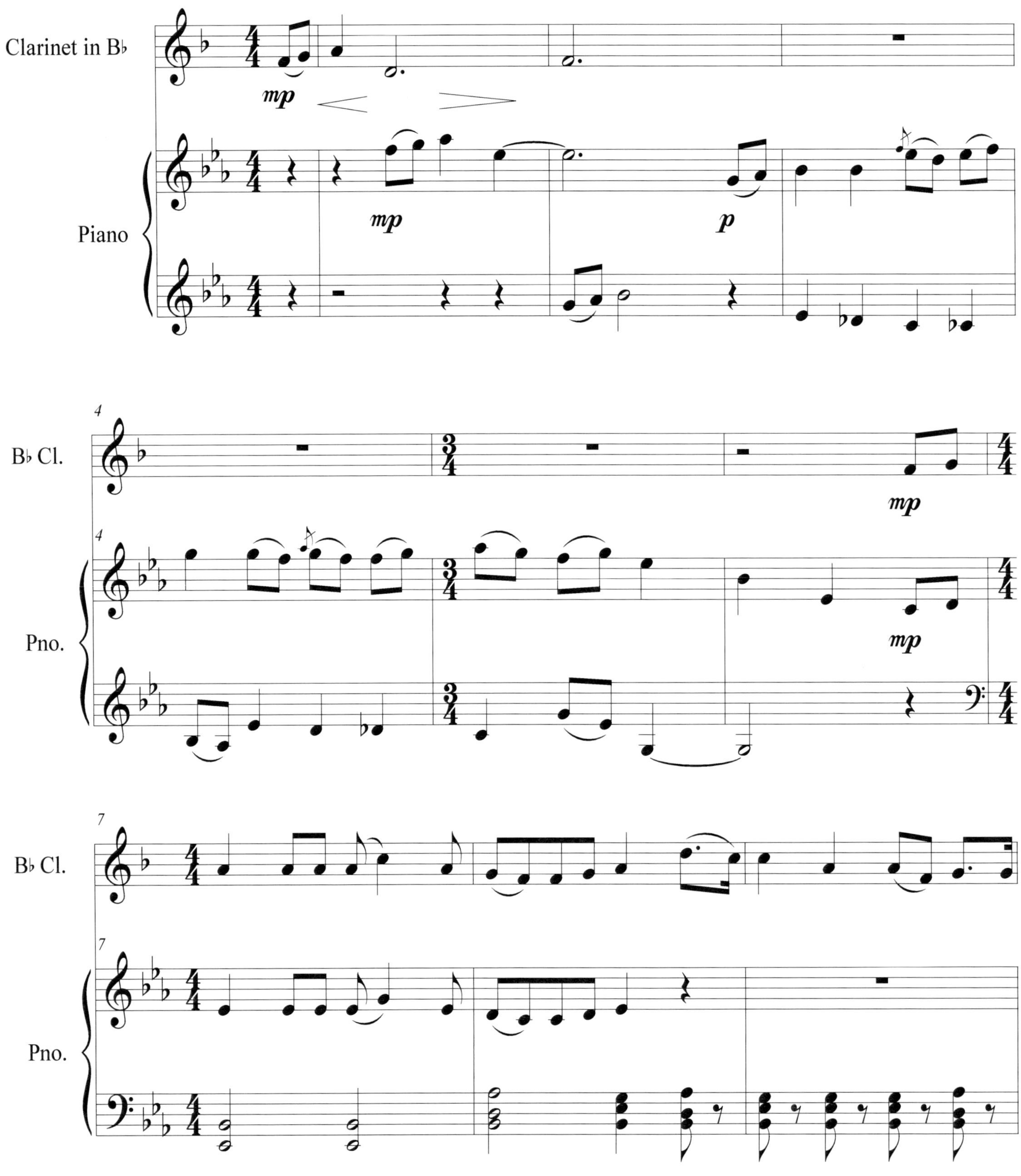

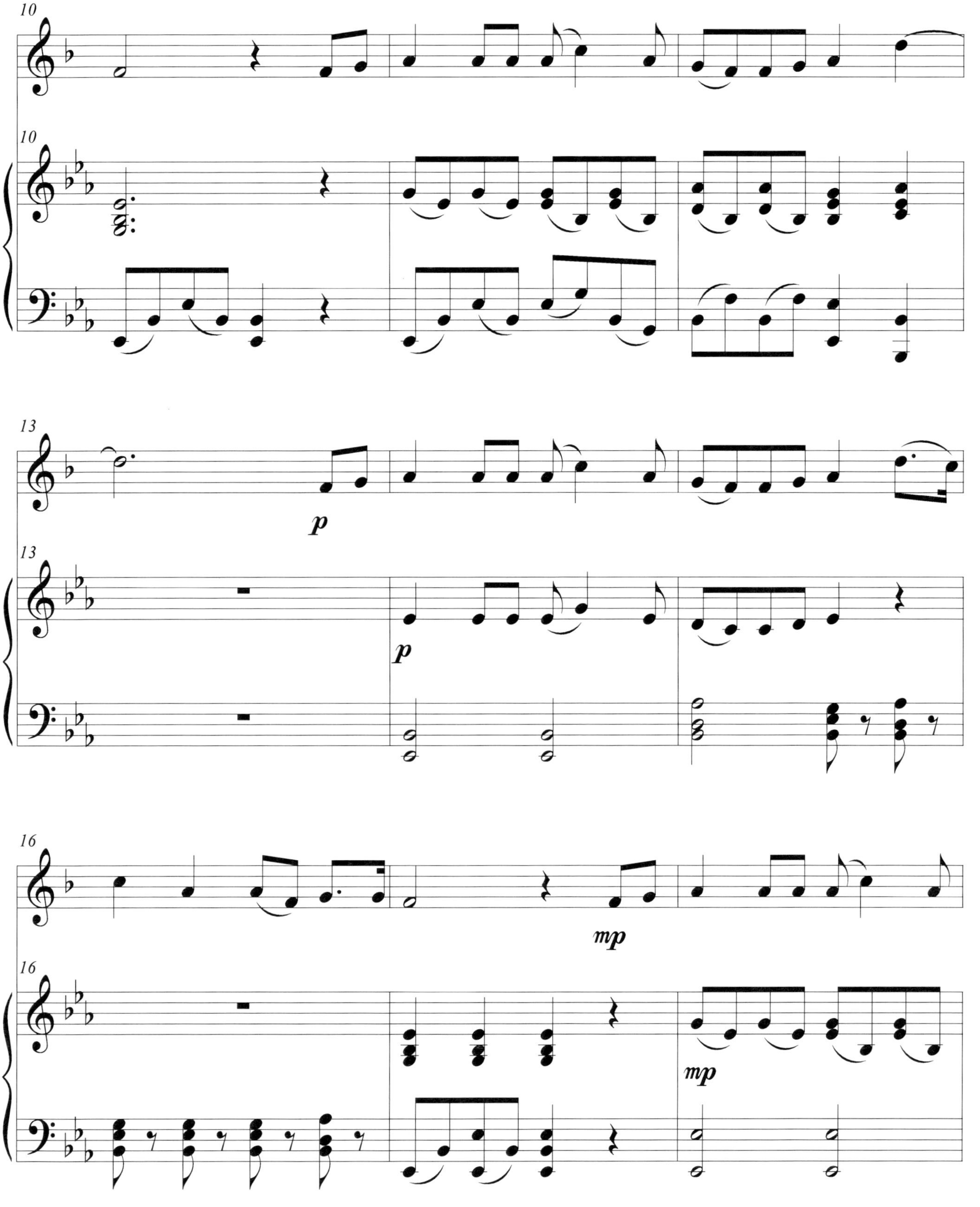

B♭ Cl.
Pno.
p
mp

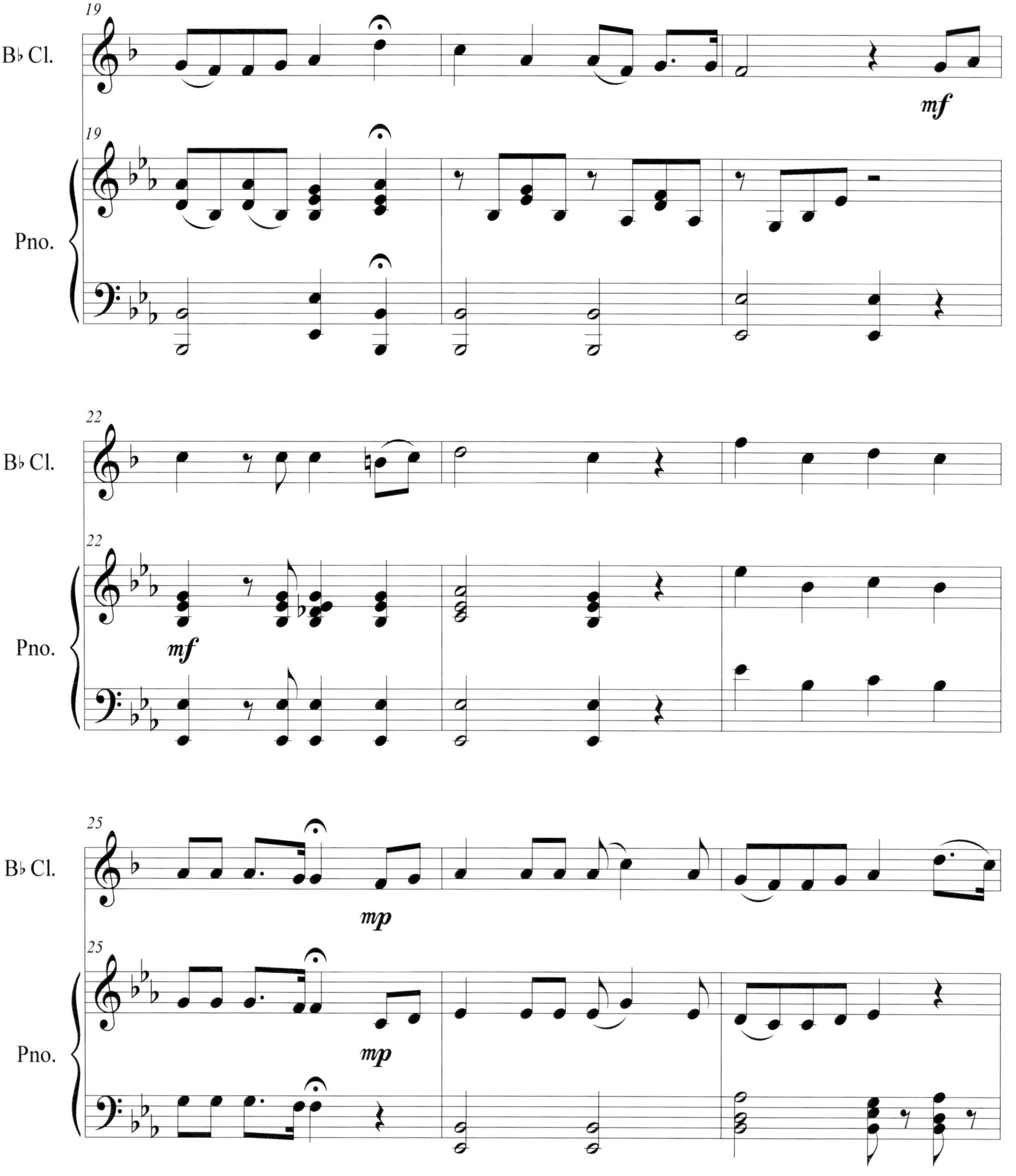
B♭ Cl.
Pno.
mf
mf
mp
mp

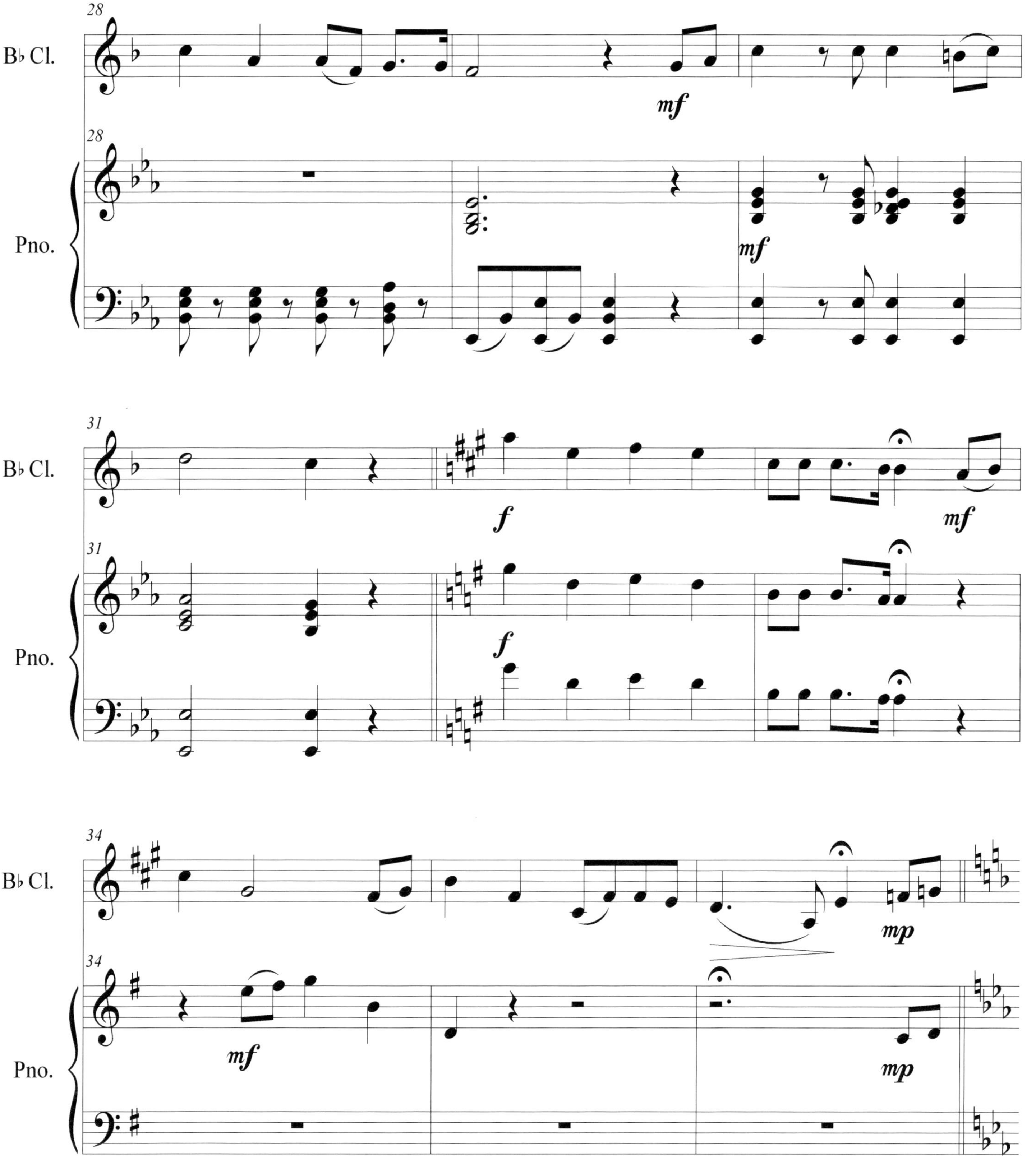
B♭ Cl.
Pno.
mf
f
mp

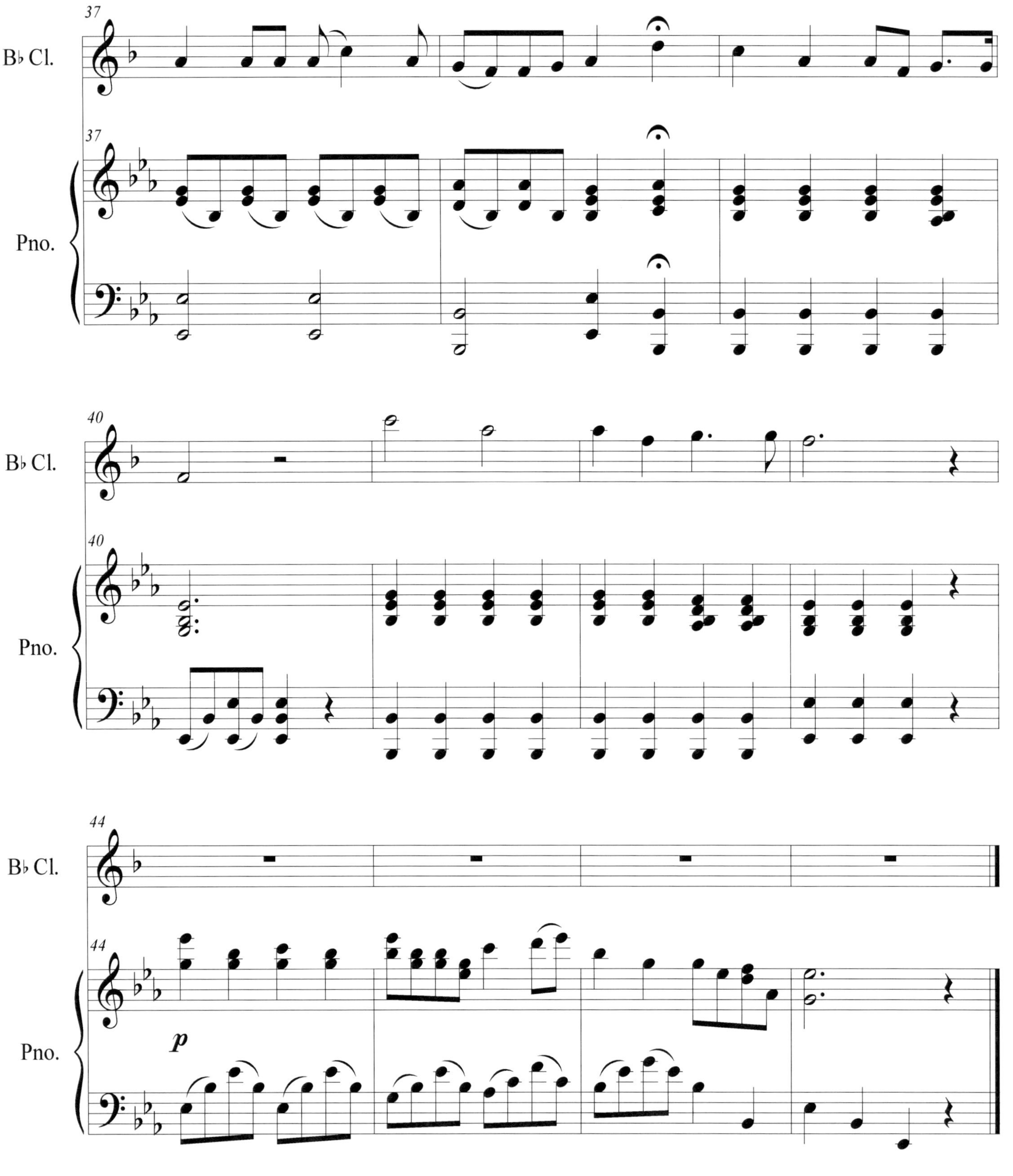
B♭ Cl.
Pno.
37
40
44
p

*This page has been left blank to avoid an awkward page turn.*

# *Camptown Races - Reel*

Stephen Foster

Arr. James Marshall

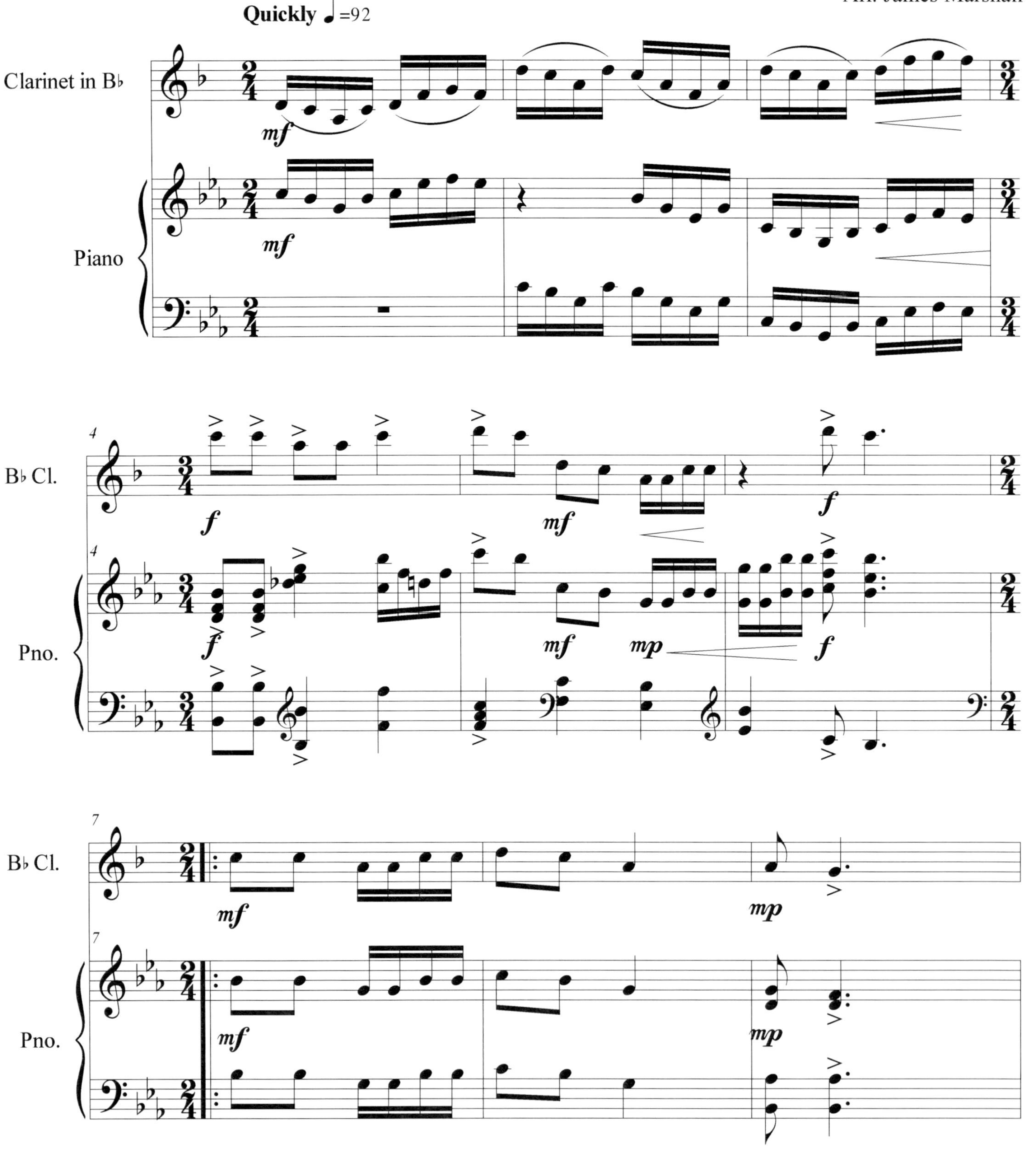

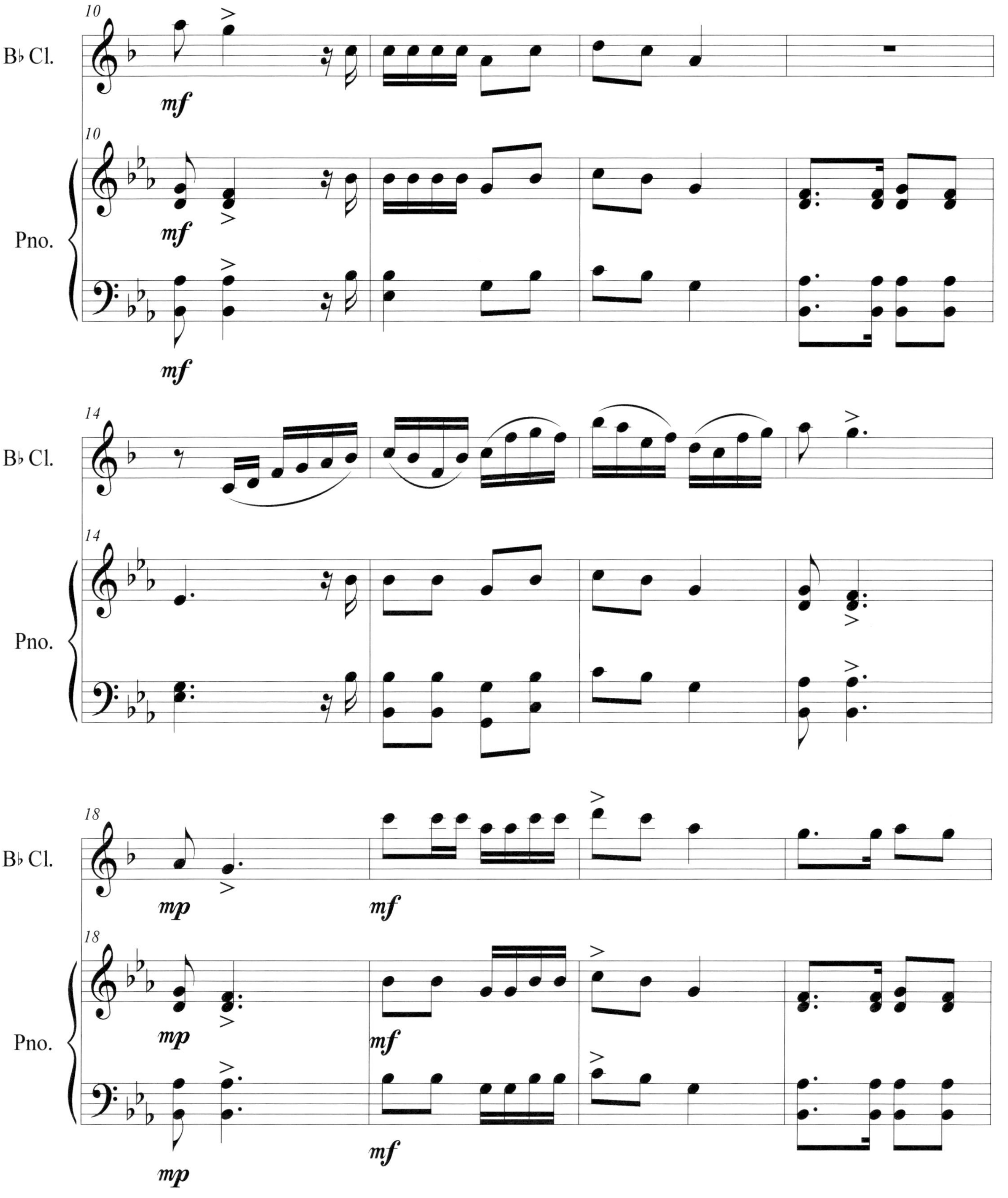
B♭ Cl.
Pno.
mf
mp
10
14
18

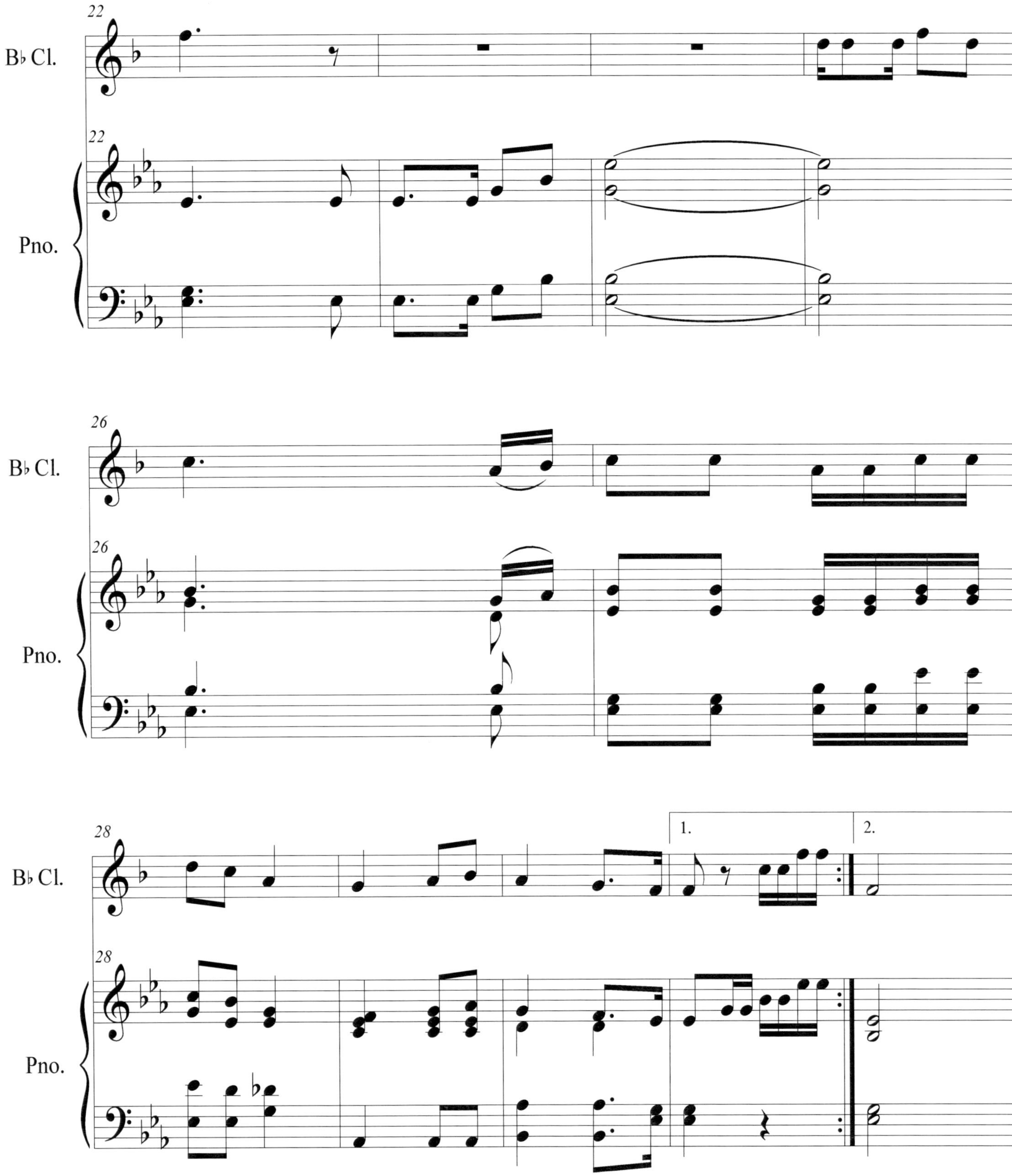
22
B♭ Cl.
22
Pno.
26
B♭ Cl.
26
Pno.
28
1.
2.
B♭ Cl.
28
Pno.

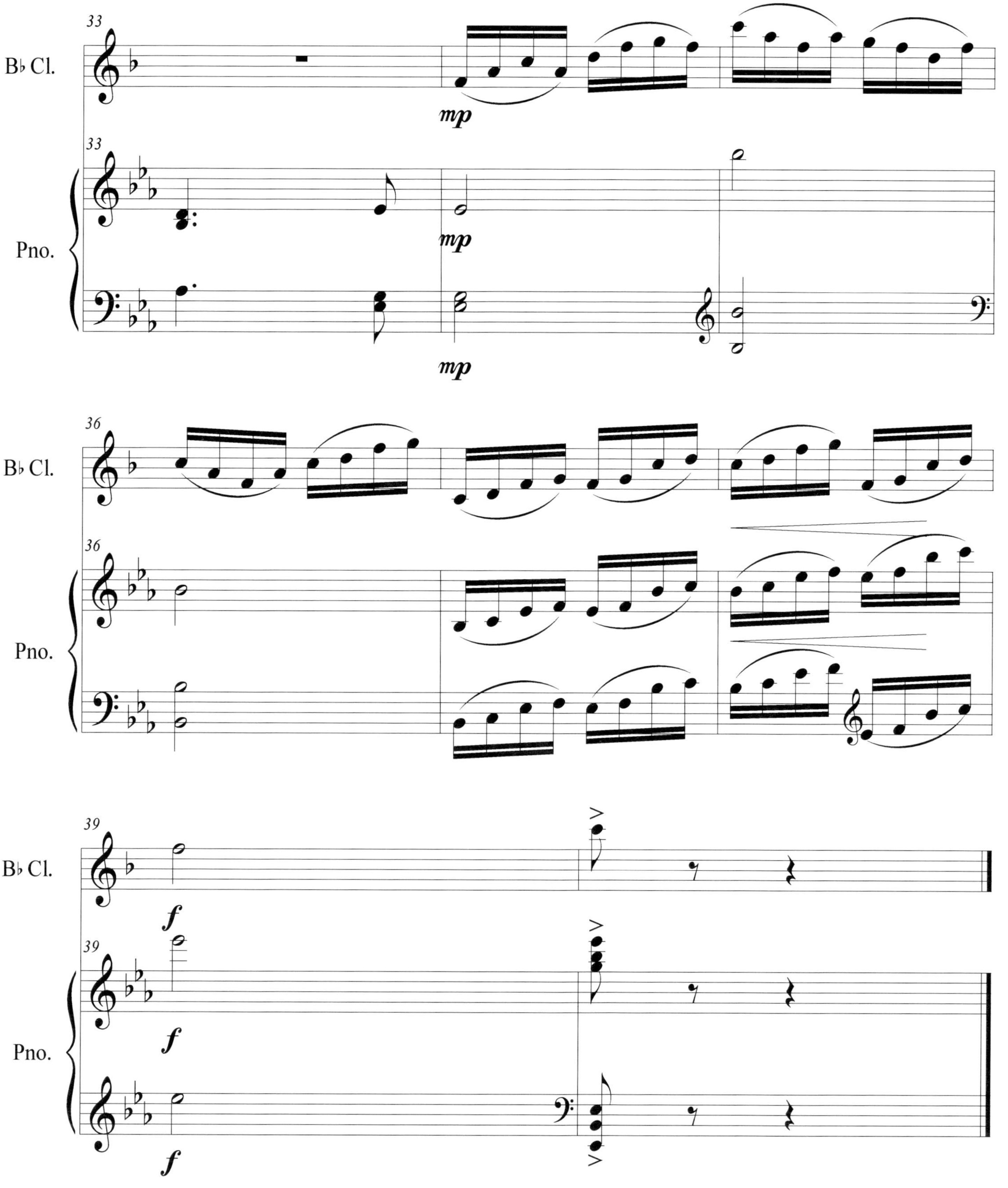
33
B♭ Cl.
Pno.
mp
36
39
f

# *Anthem*

Sacred Harp

Arr. James Marshall

**Uplifting, gently lilting** ♩ = 90

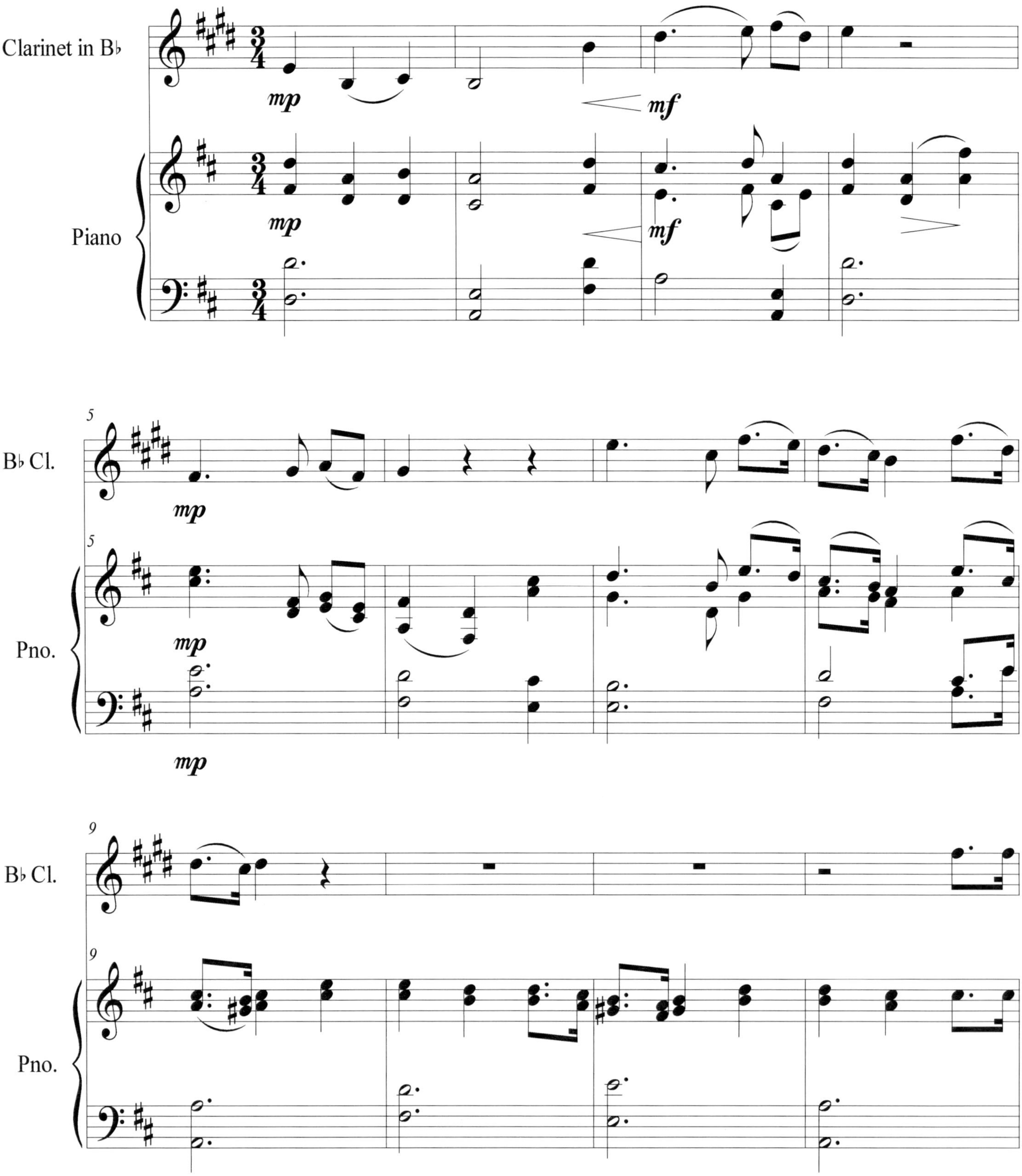

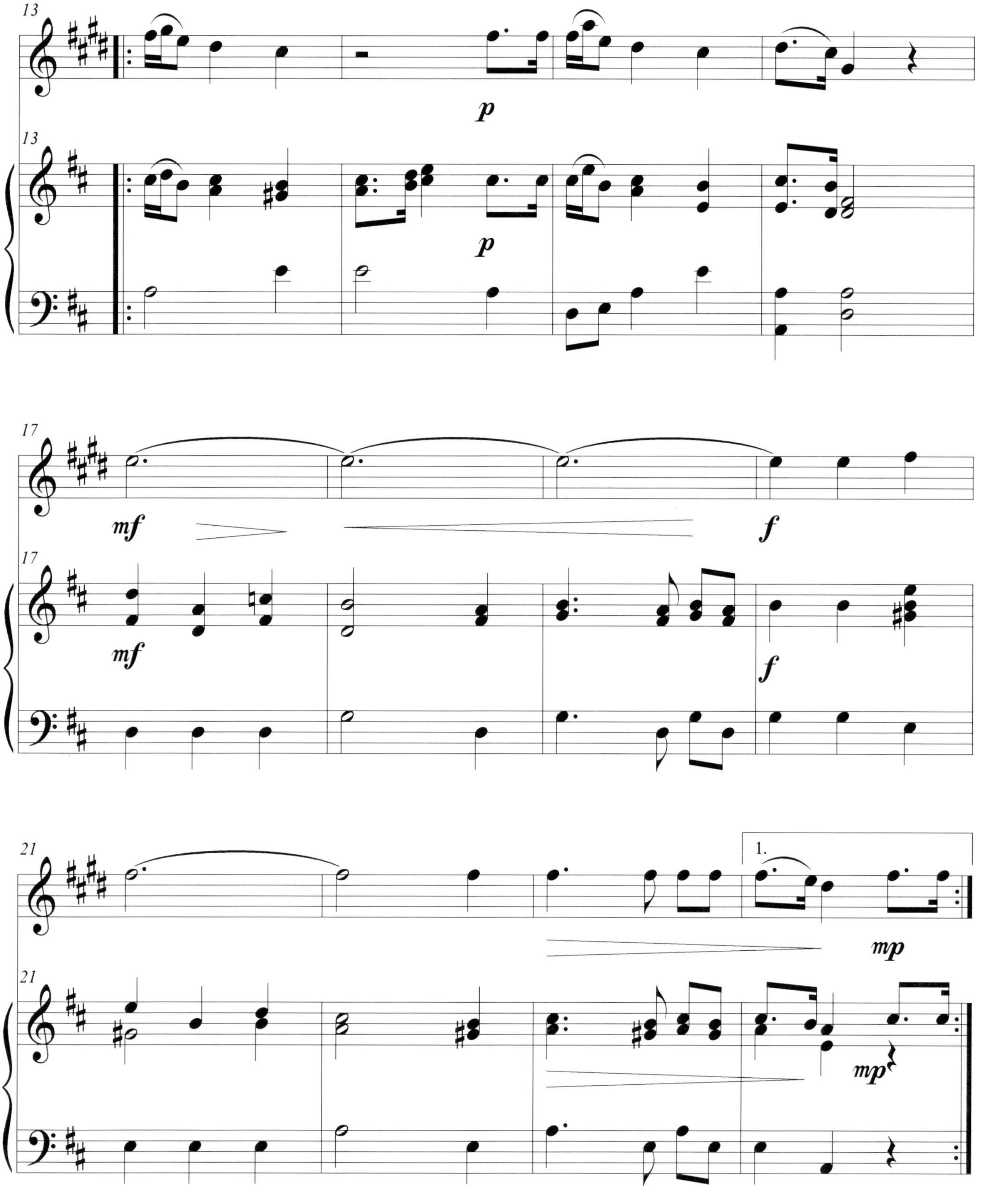
B♭ Cl.
Pno.

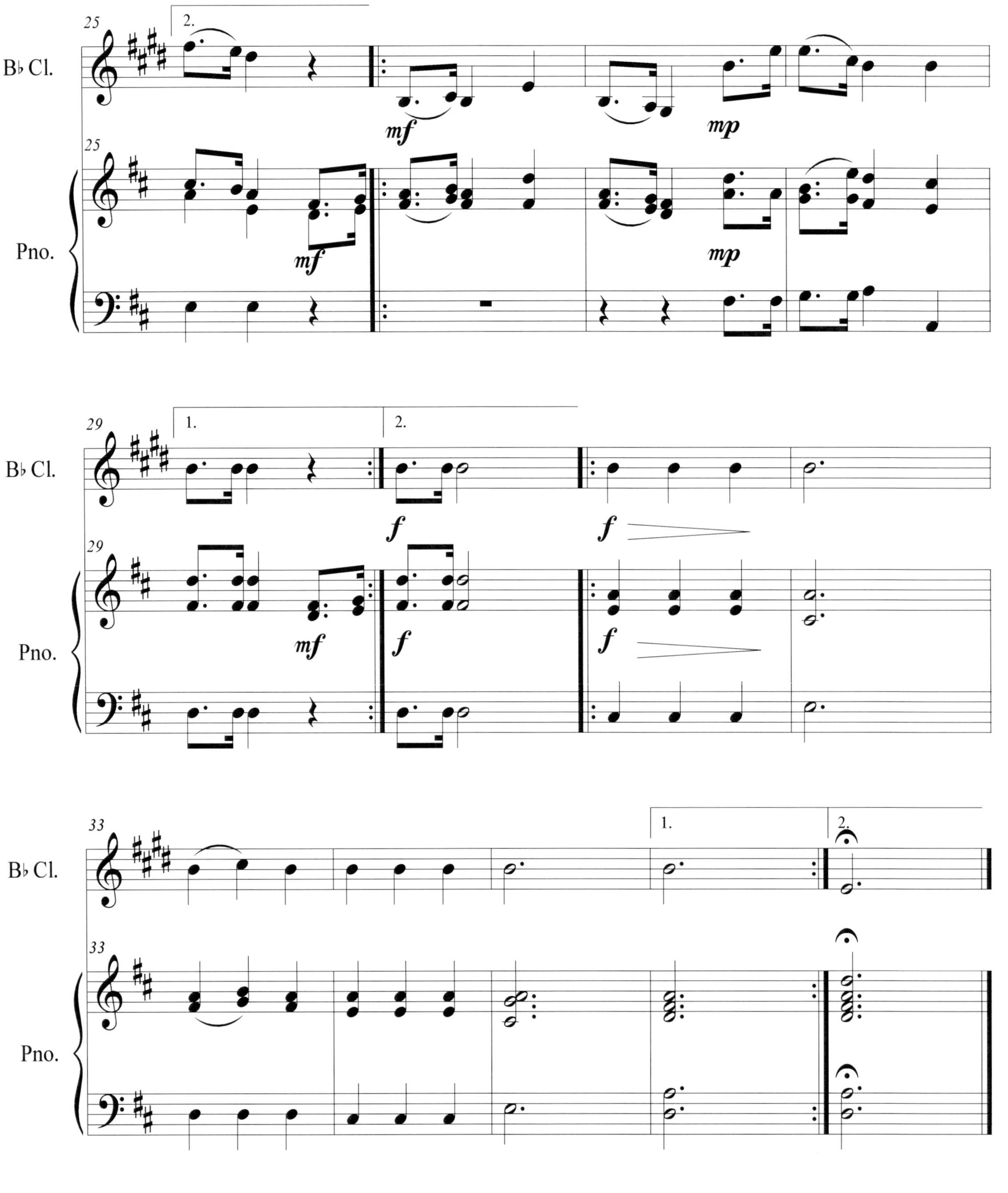

B♭ Cl.
Pno.
mf
mp
f

*This page has been left blank to avoid an awkward page turn.*

# *Poor Wayfaring Stranger*

American Folk Song

Arr. James Marshall

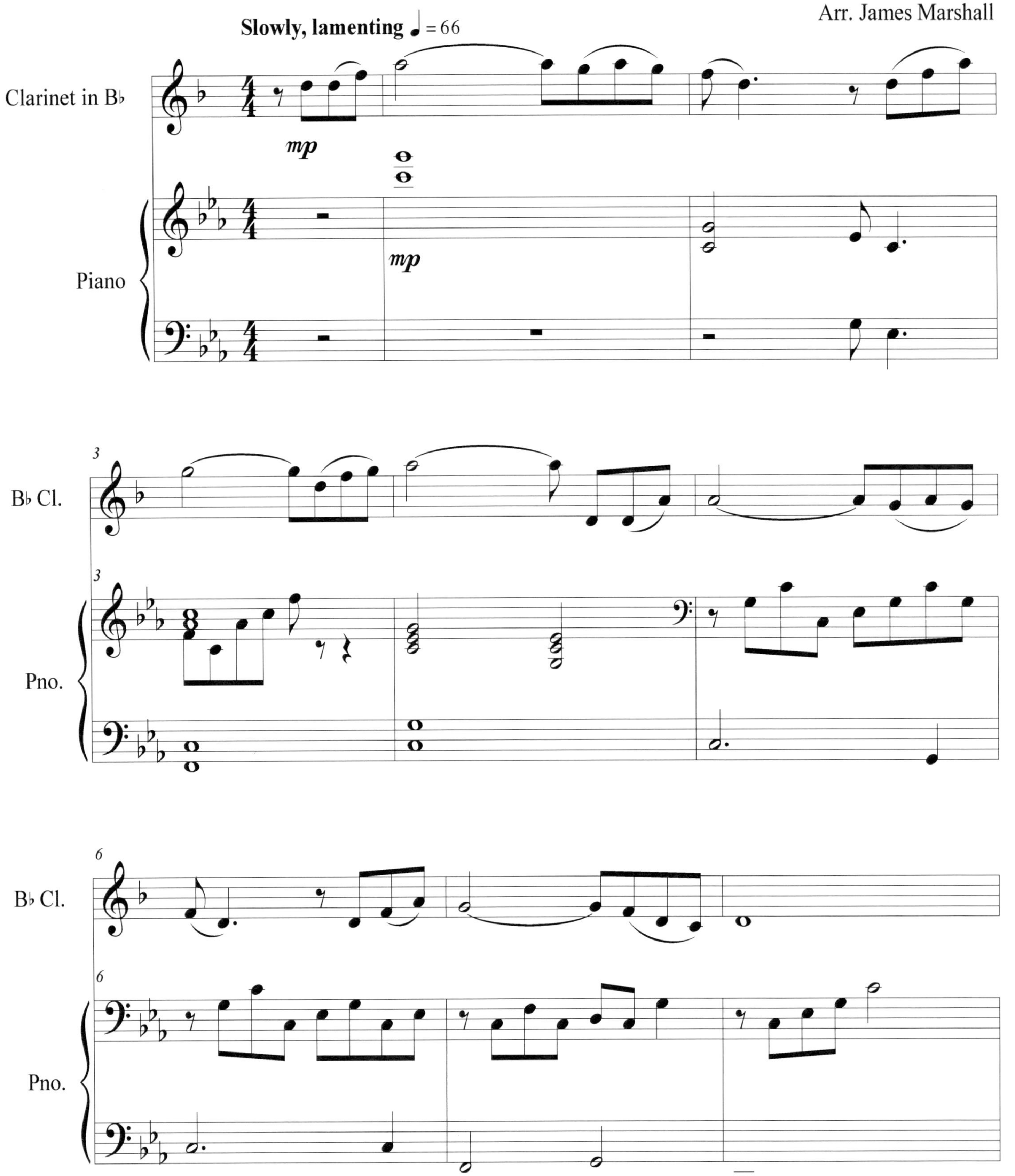

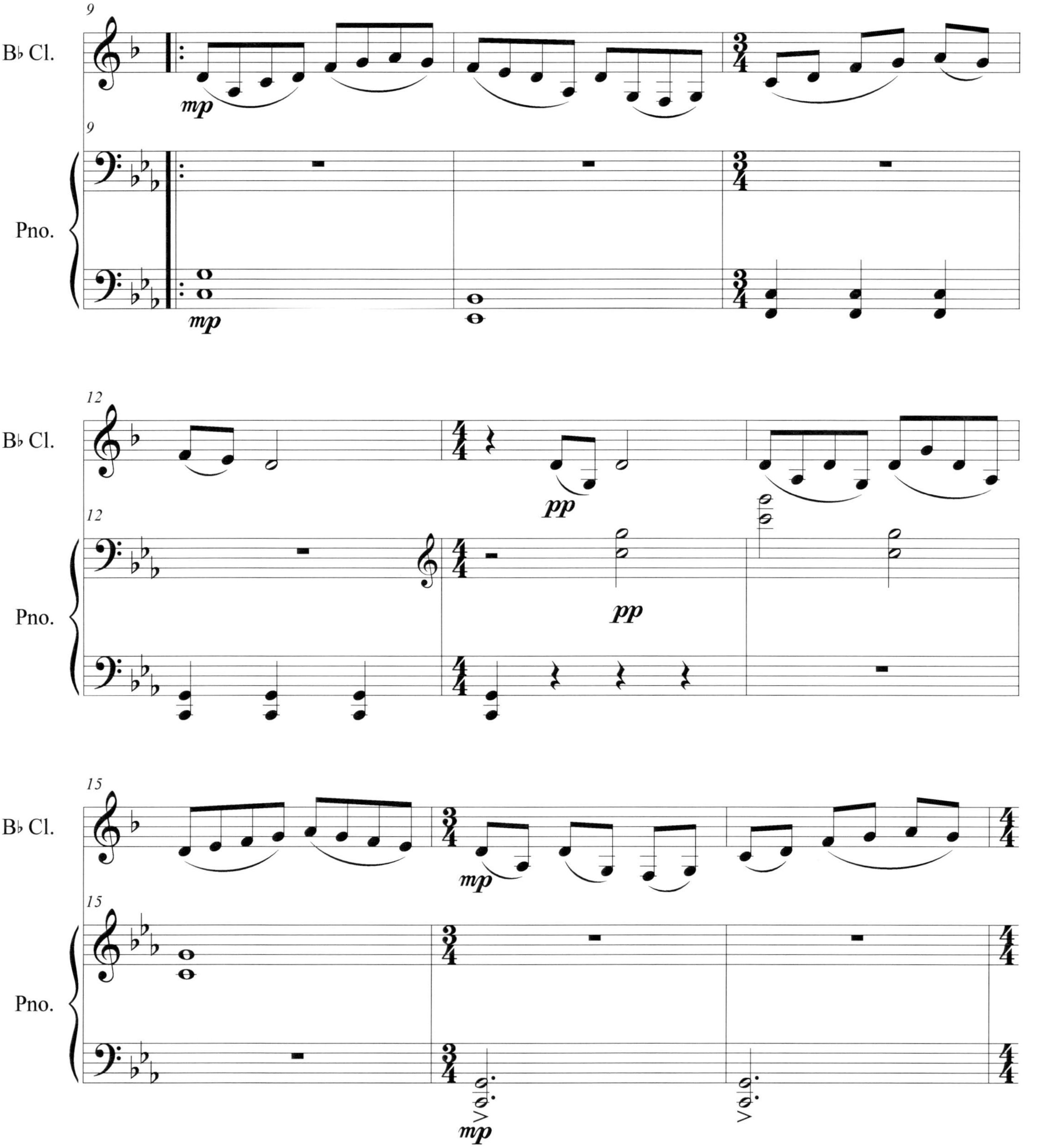
9
B♭ Cl.
mp
9
Pno.
mp
12
B♭ Cl.
pp
12
Pno.
pp
15
B♭ Cl.
mp
15
Pno.
mp

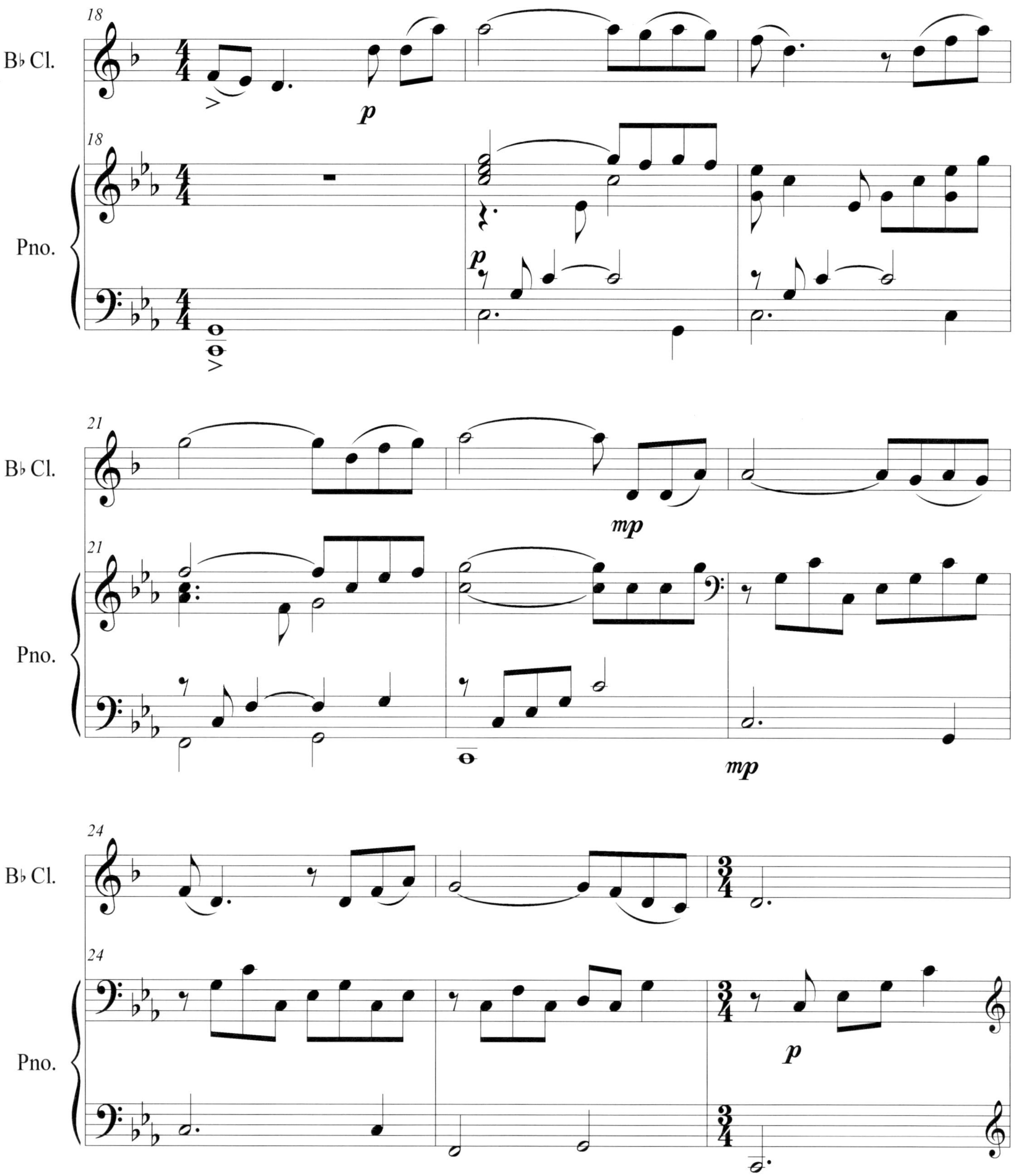
B♭ Cl.
Pno.
18
21
24
p
mp

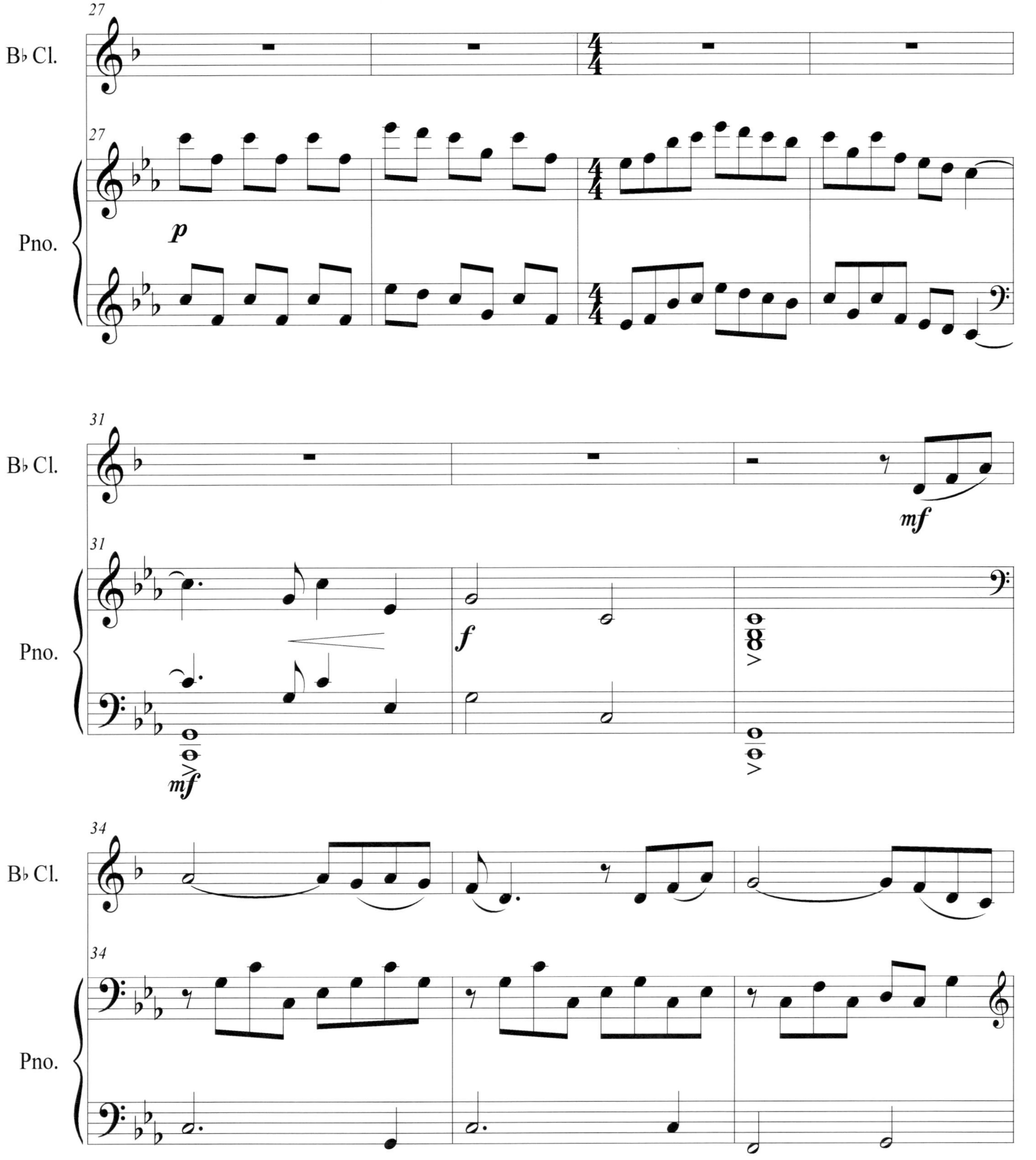
27
B♭ Cl.
Pno.
p
31
mf
f
34

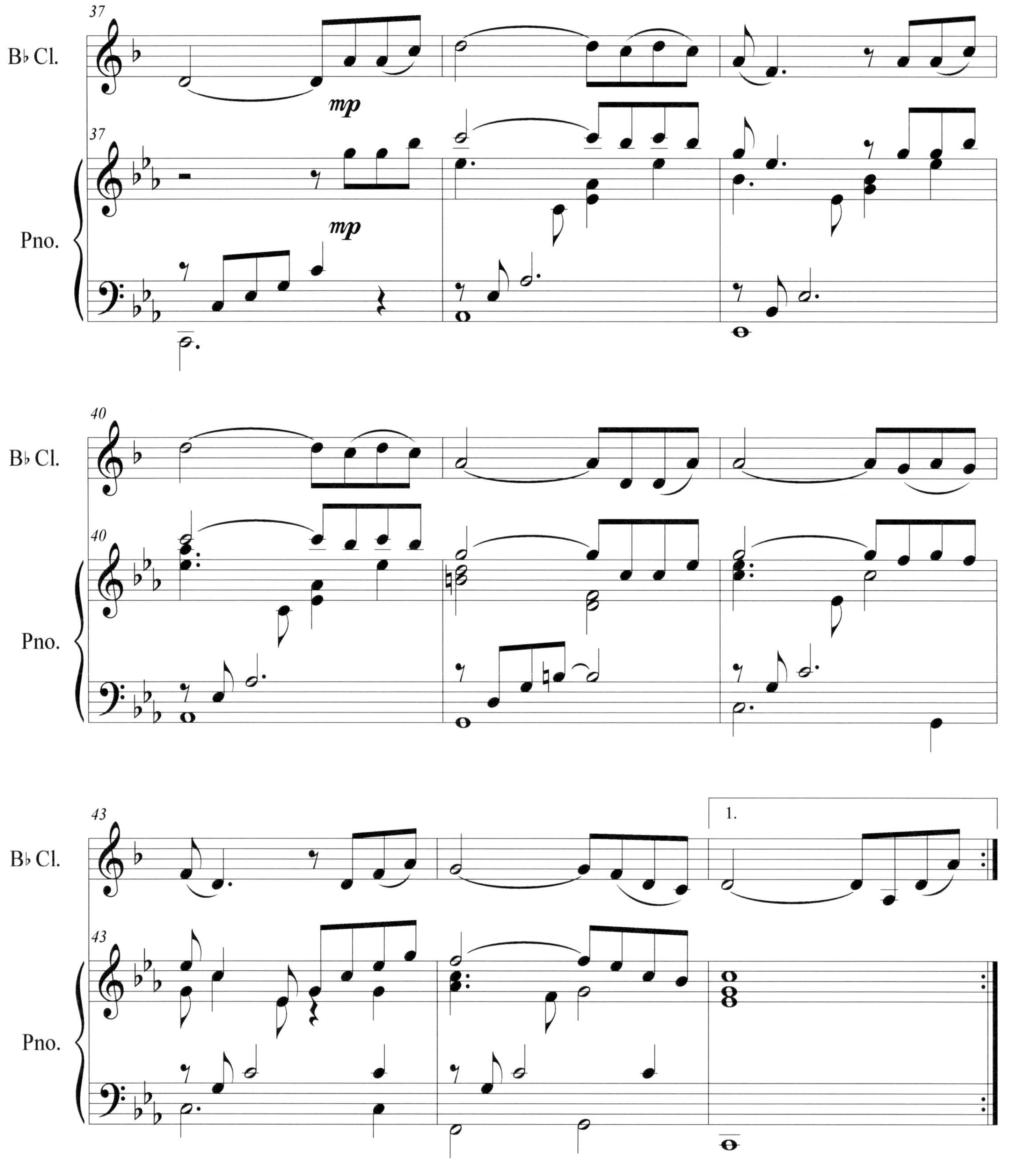

B♭ Cl.
Pno.
mp
mp
B♭ Cl.
Pno.
B♭ Cl.
Pno.
1.

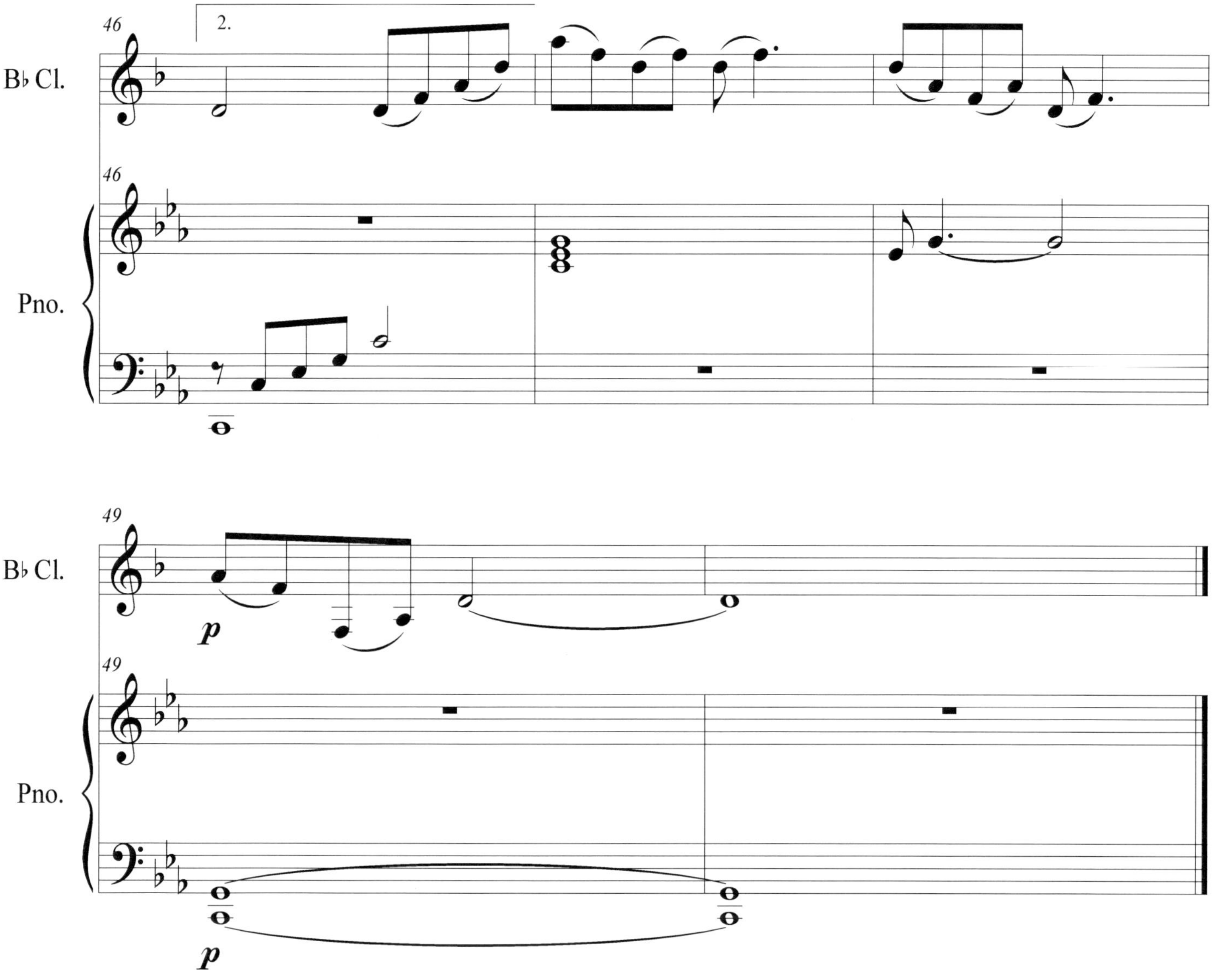
46
2.
B♭ Cl.
Pno.
49
p
p

# *Aura Lee*

Civil War Song

Arr. James Marshall

**Gently** ♩ = 92

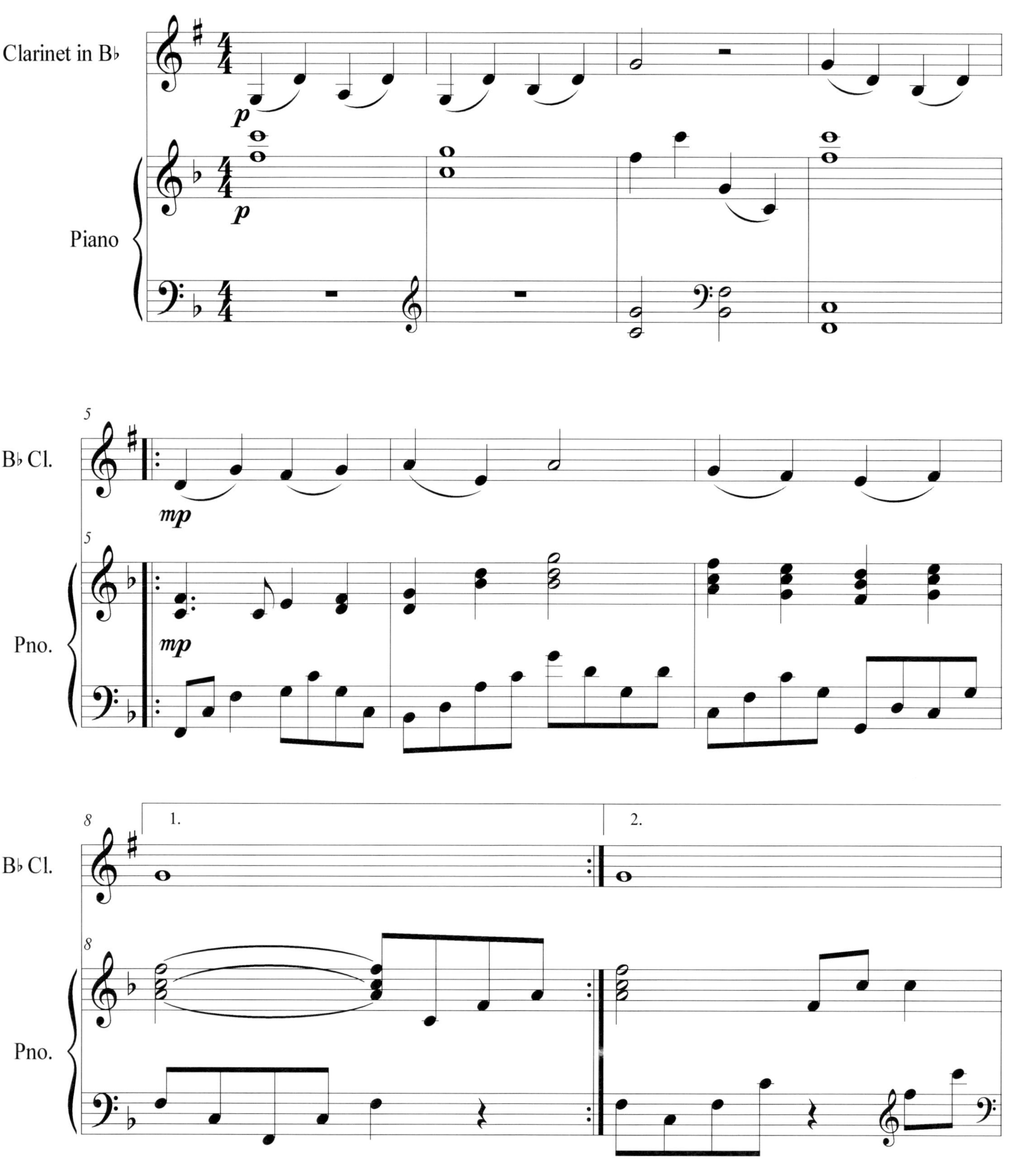

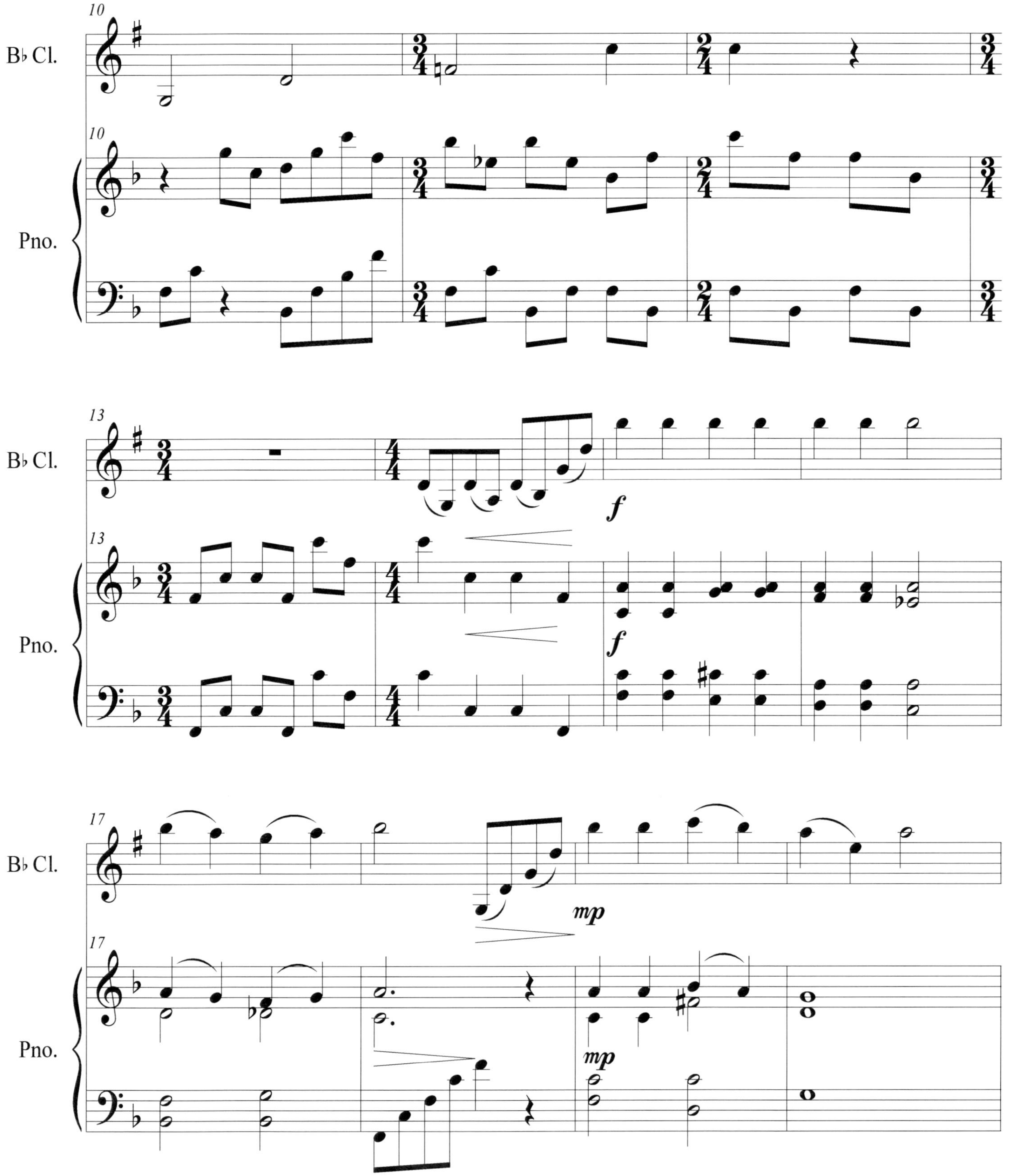
B♭ Cl.
Pno.
10
13
17
f
mp

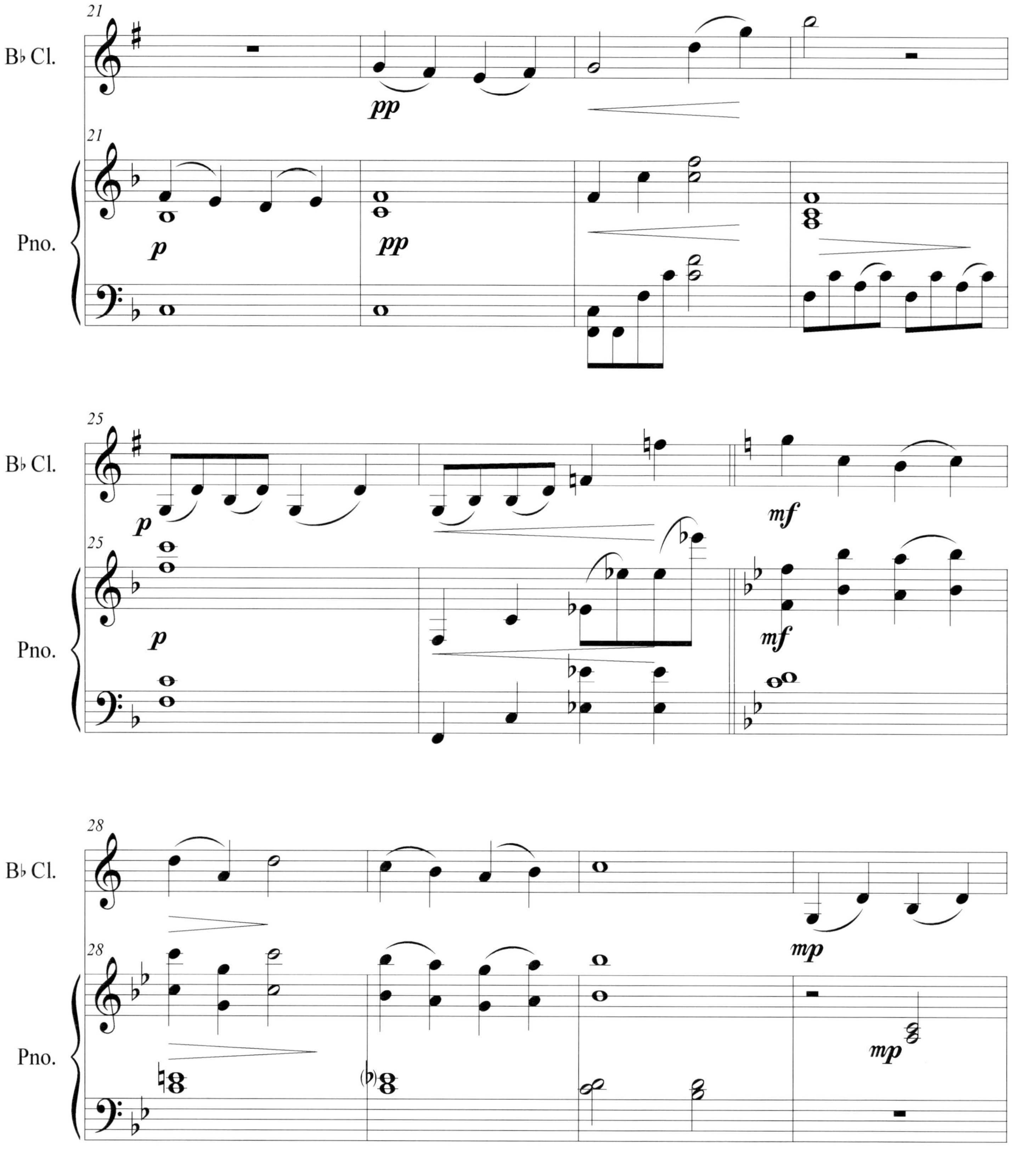
21
B♭ Cl.
pp
21
Pno.
p
pp
25
B♭ Cl.
p
mf
25
Pno.
p
mf
28
B♭ Cl.
mp
28
Pno.
mp

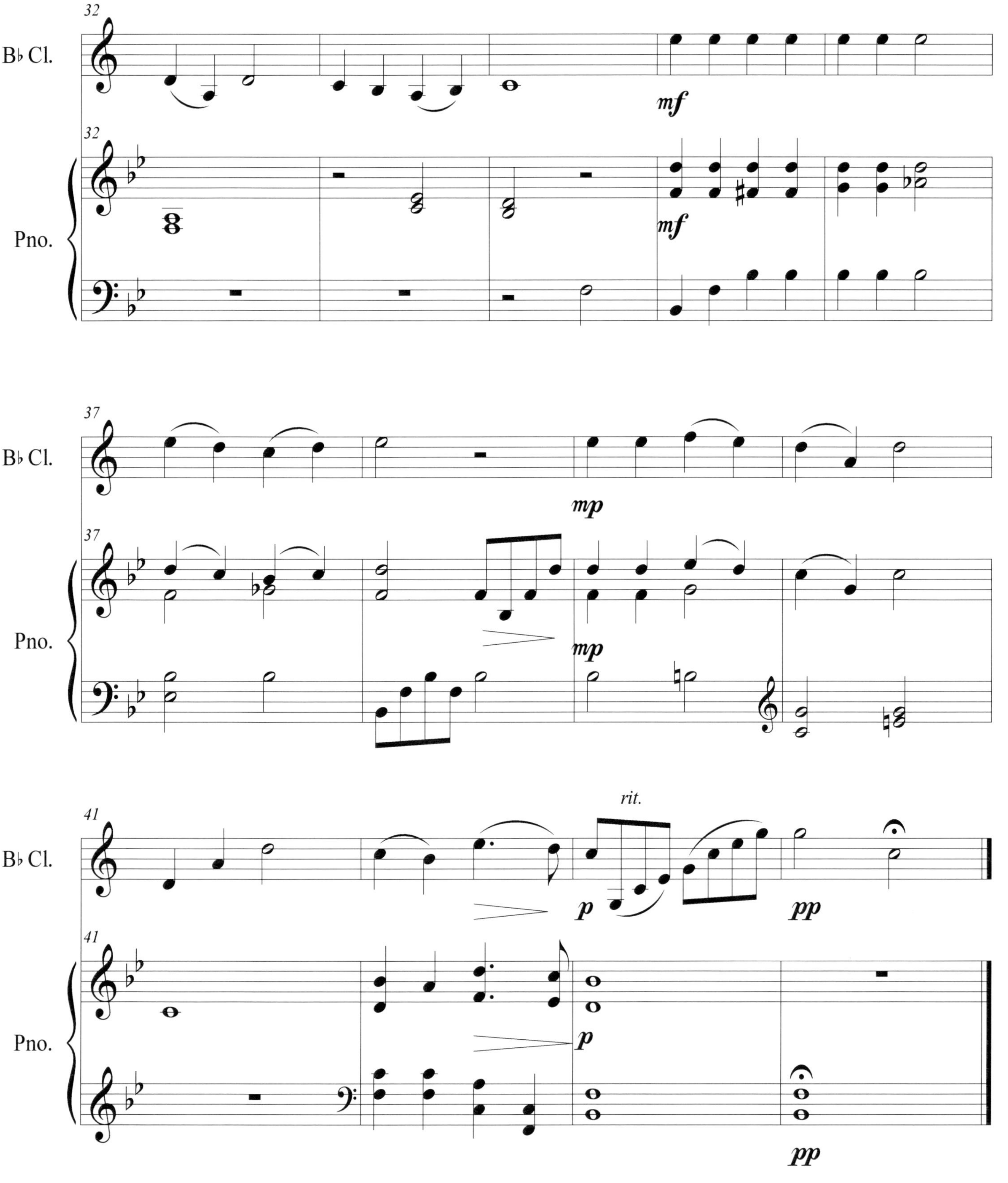
B♭ Cl.
Pno.
mf
mp
rit.
p
pp

# *Black Is the Color of My True Love's Hair*

Southern Appalachian Folk Song

Arr. James Marshall

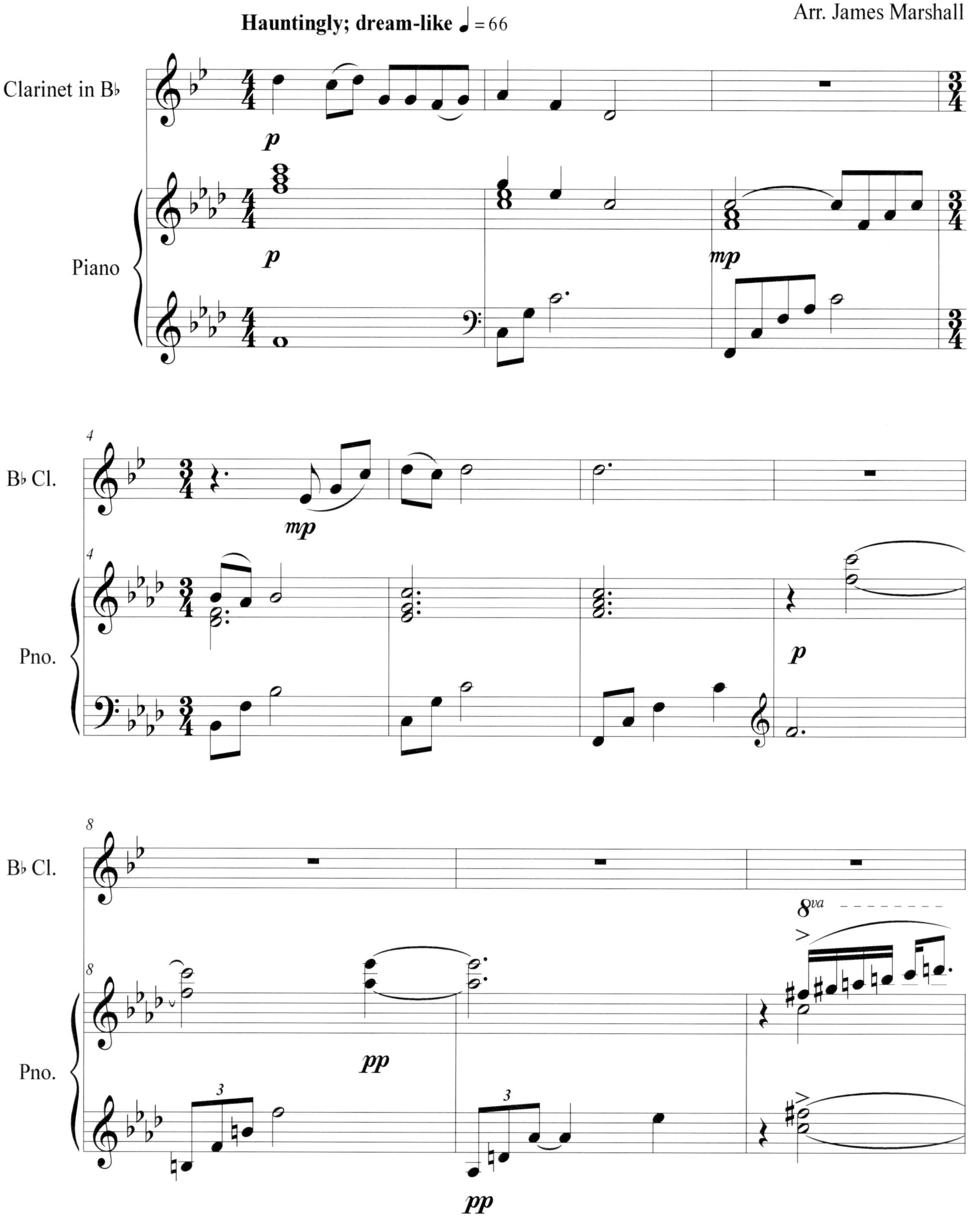

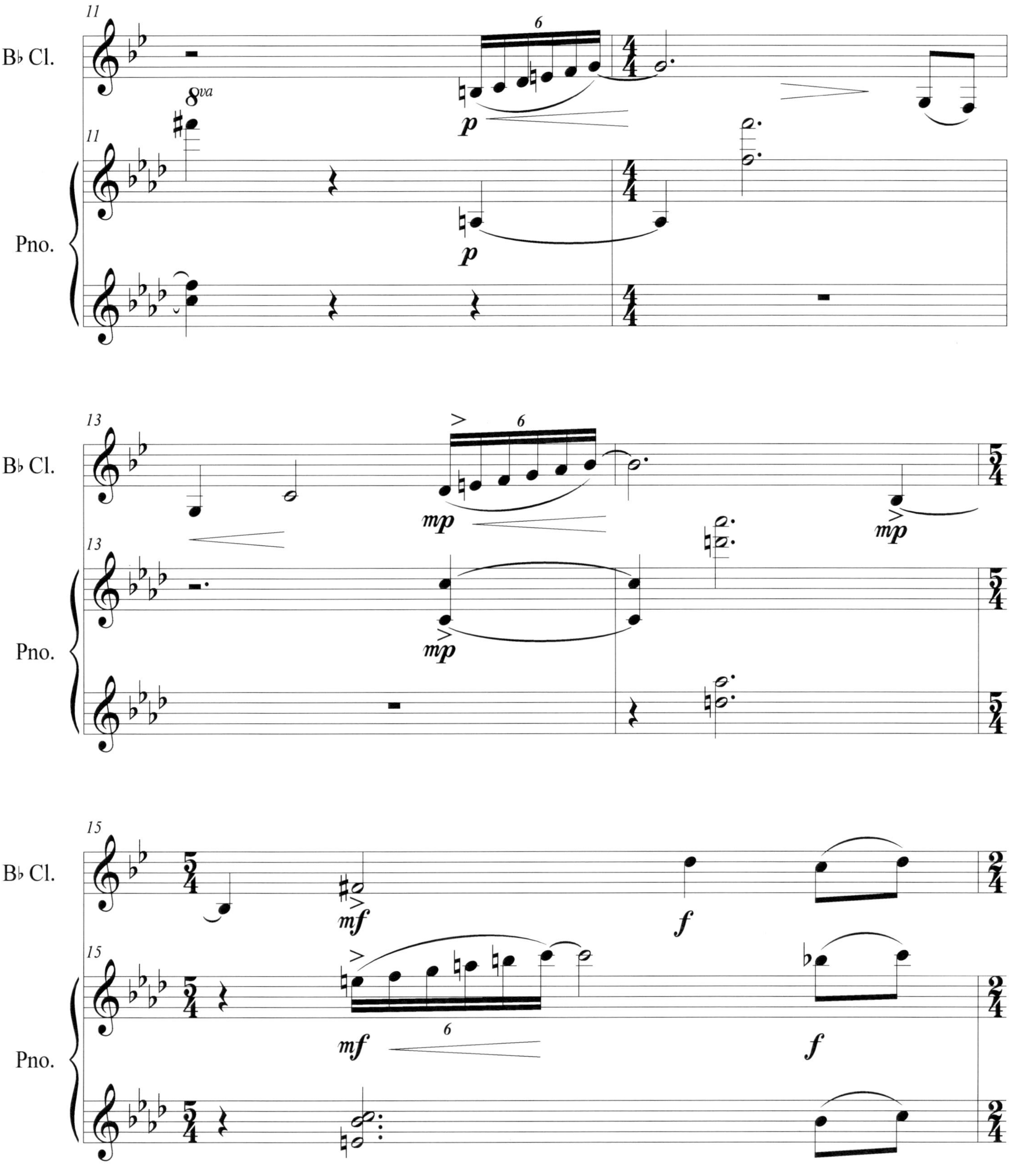
B♭ Cl.
Pno.
8va
6
p
mp
mf
f

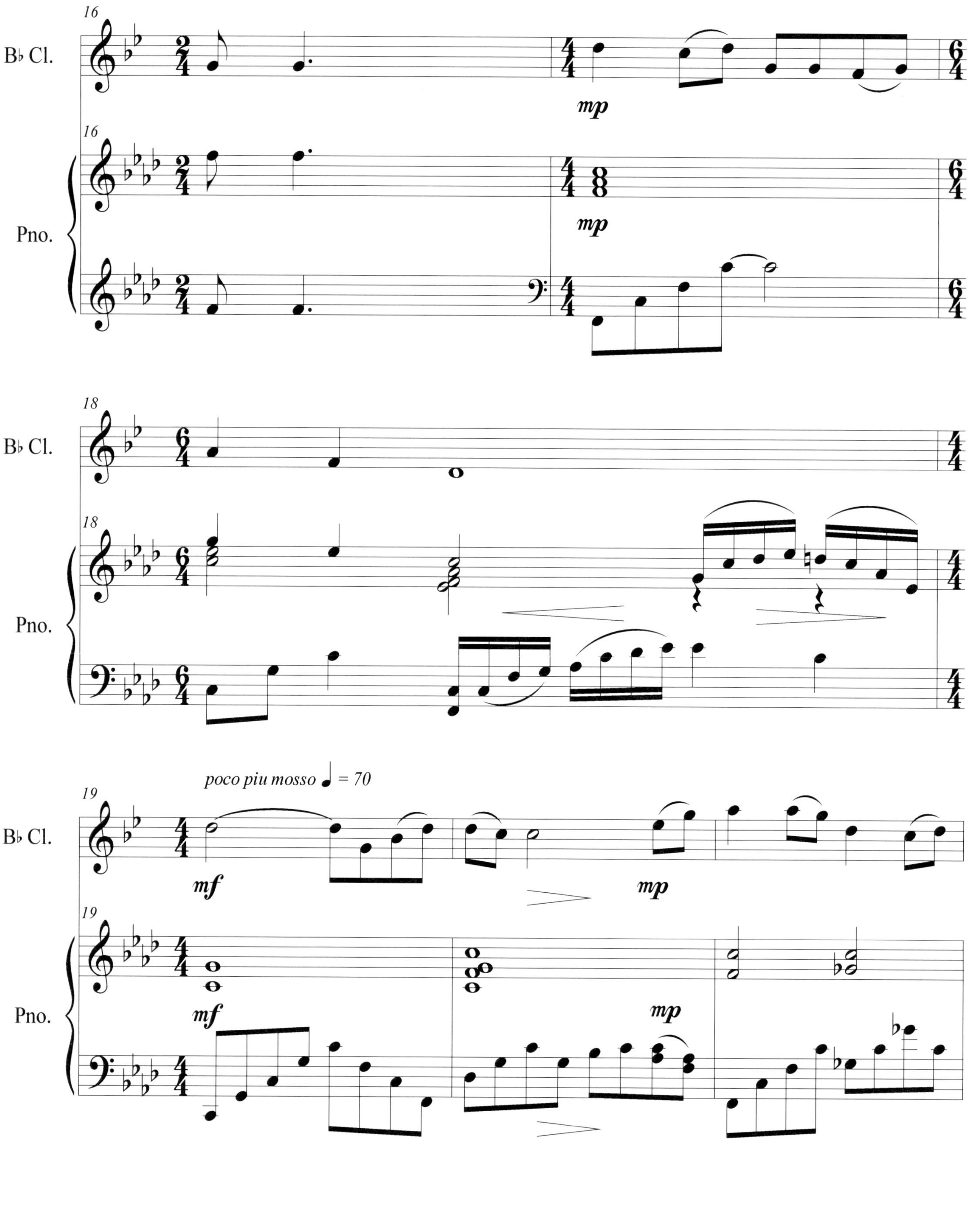
16
B♭ Cl.
mp
16
Pno.
mp
18
B♭ Cl.
18
Pno.
poco piu mosso ♩ = 70
19
B♭ Cl.
mf
mp
19
Pno.
mf
mp

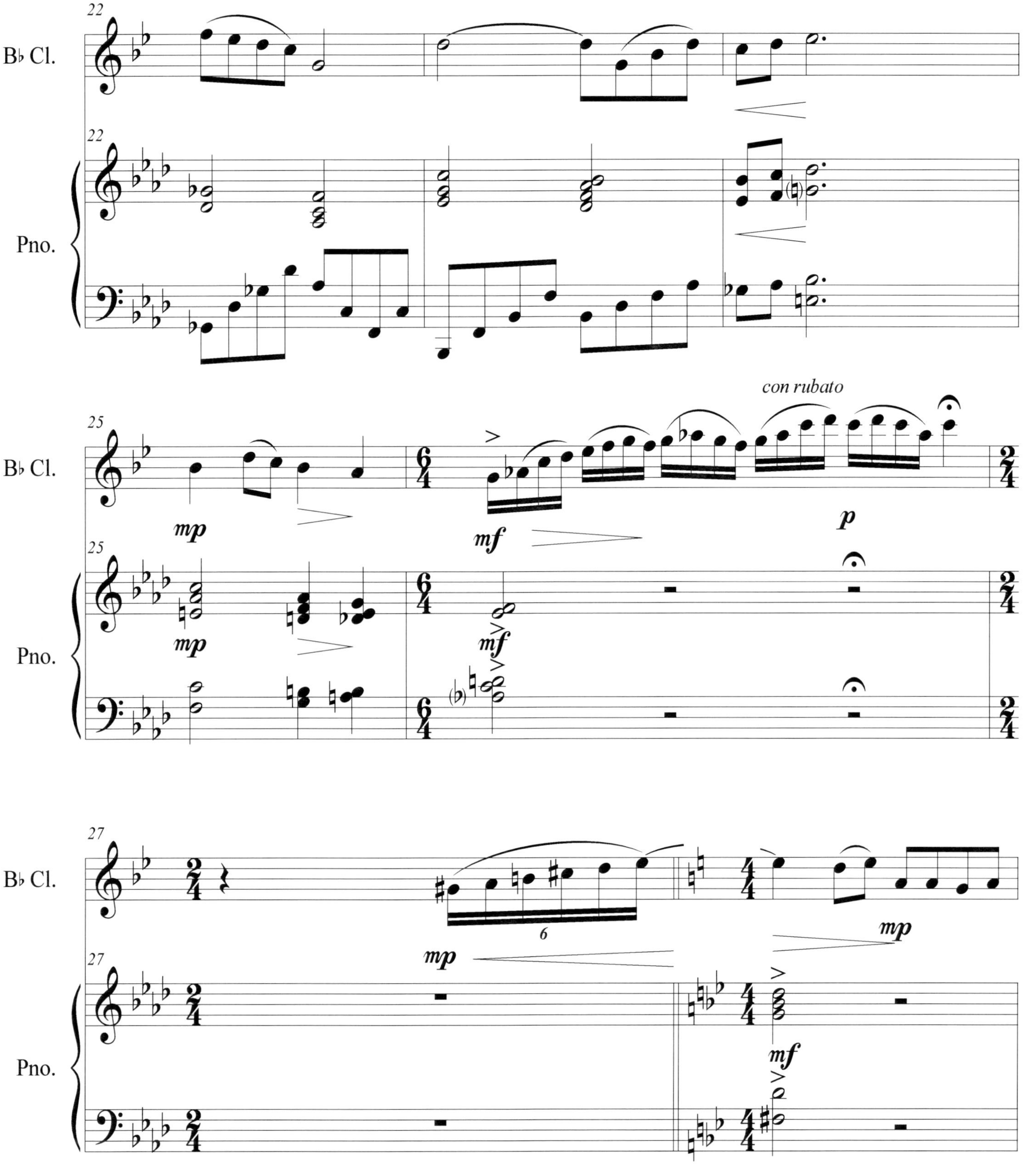
B♭ Cl.
Pno.
con rubato
mp
mf
p
mp
mp
mf
mp
mf
6

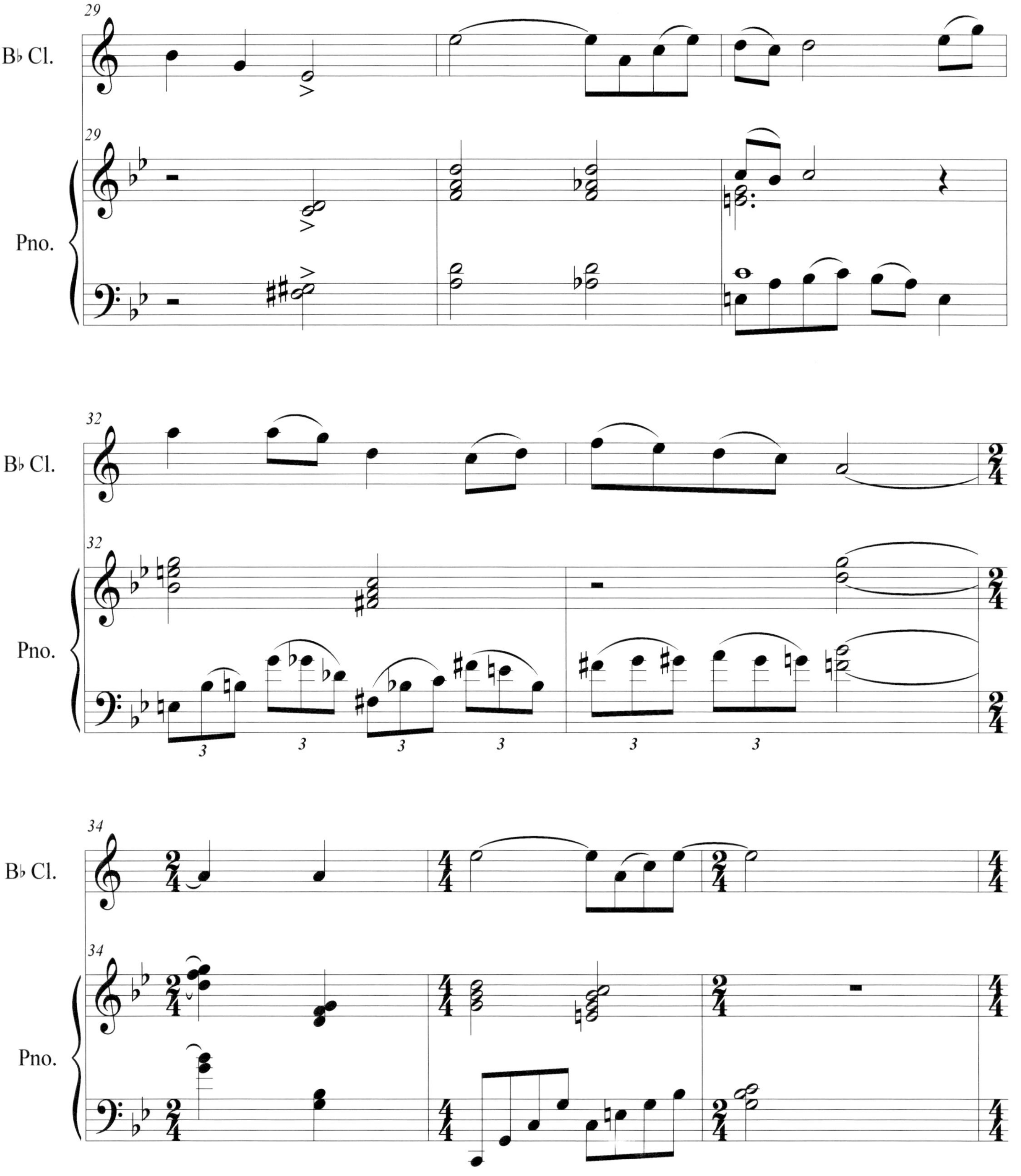
B♭ Cl.
Pno.
29
32
34
3

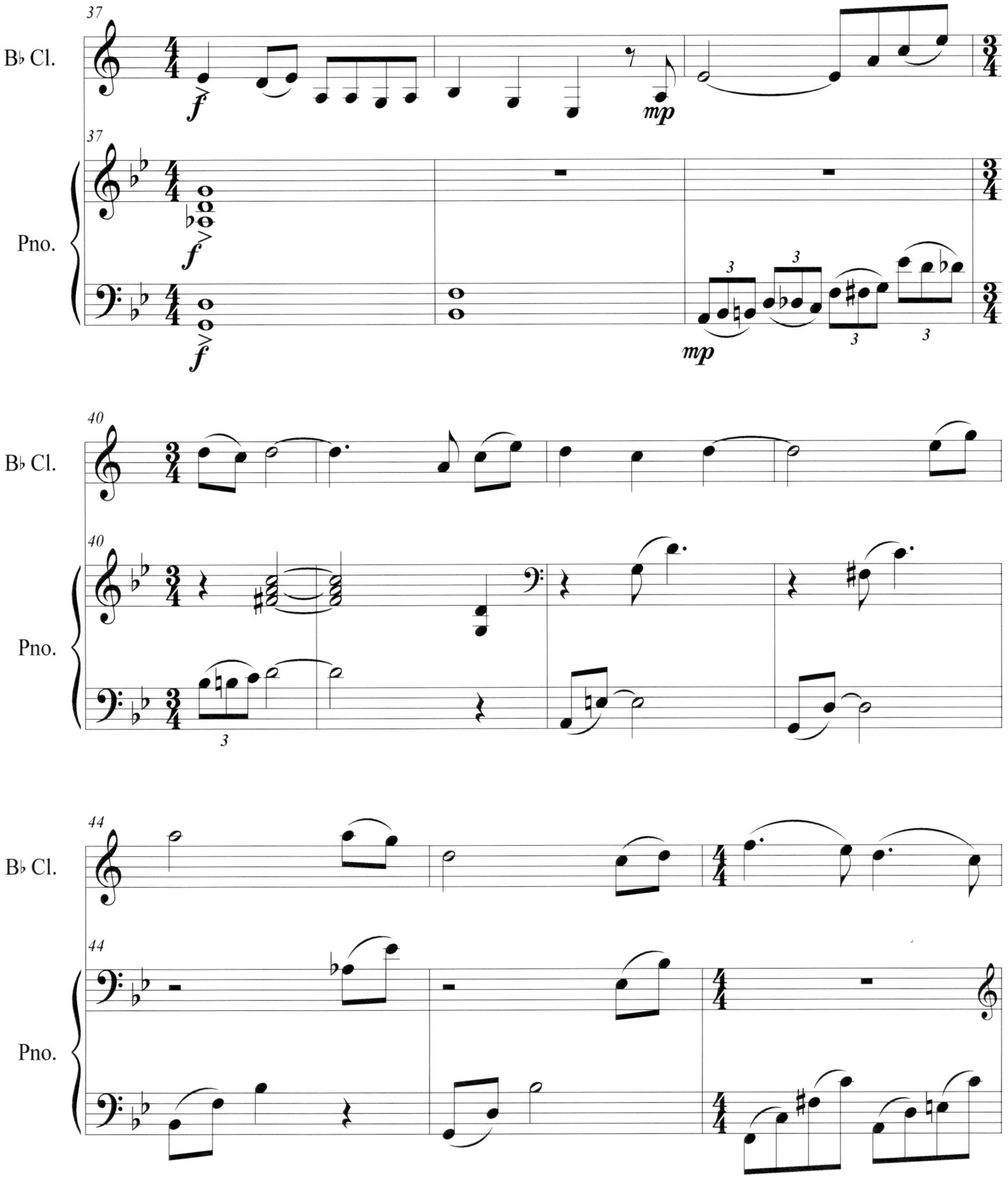
37
B♭ Cl.
f
mp
37
Pno.
f
f
mp
40
B♭ Cl.
40
Pno.
44
B♭ Cl.
44
Pno.

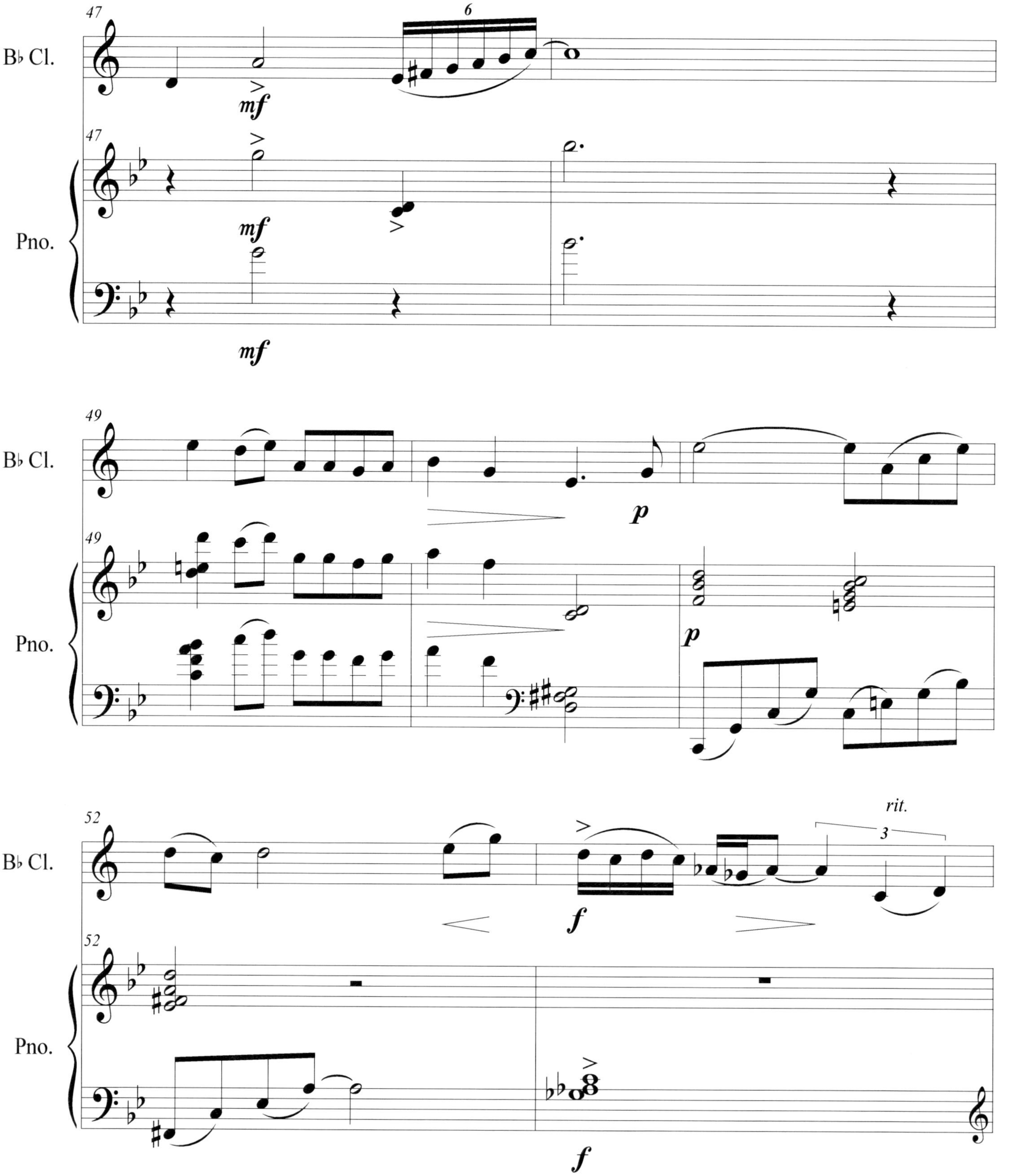
B♭ Cl.
Pno.
rit.

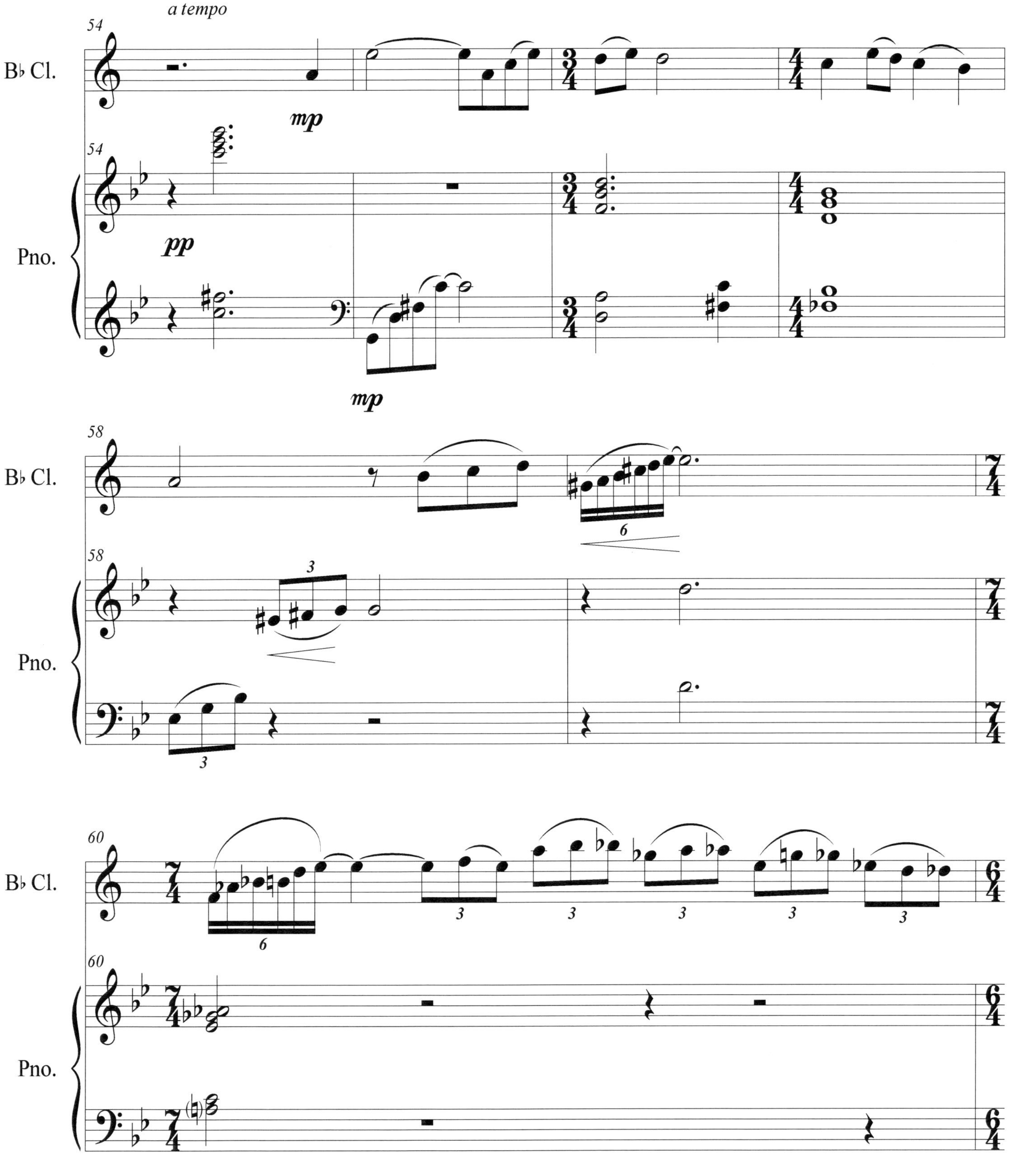
a tempo
54
B♭ Cl.
mp
54
Pno.
pp
mp
58
B♭ Cl.
6
58
3
Pno.
3
60
B♭ Cl.
6
3
3
3
3
3
60
Pno.

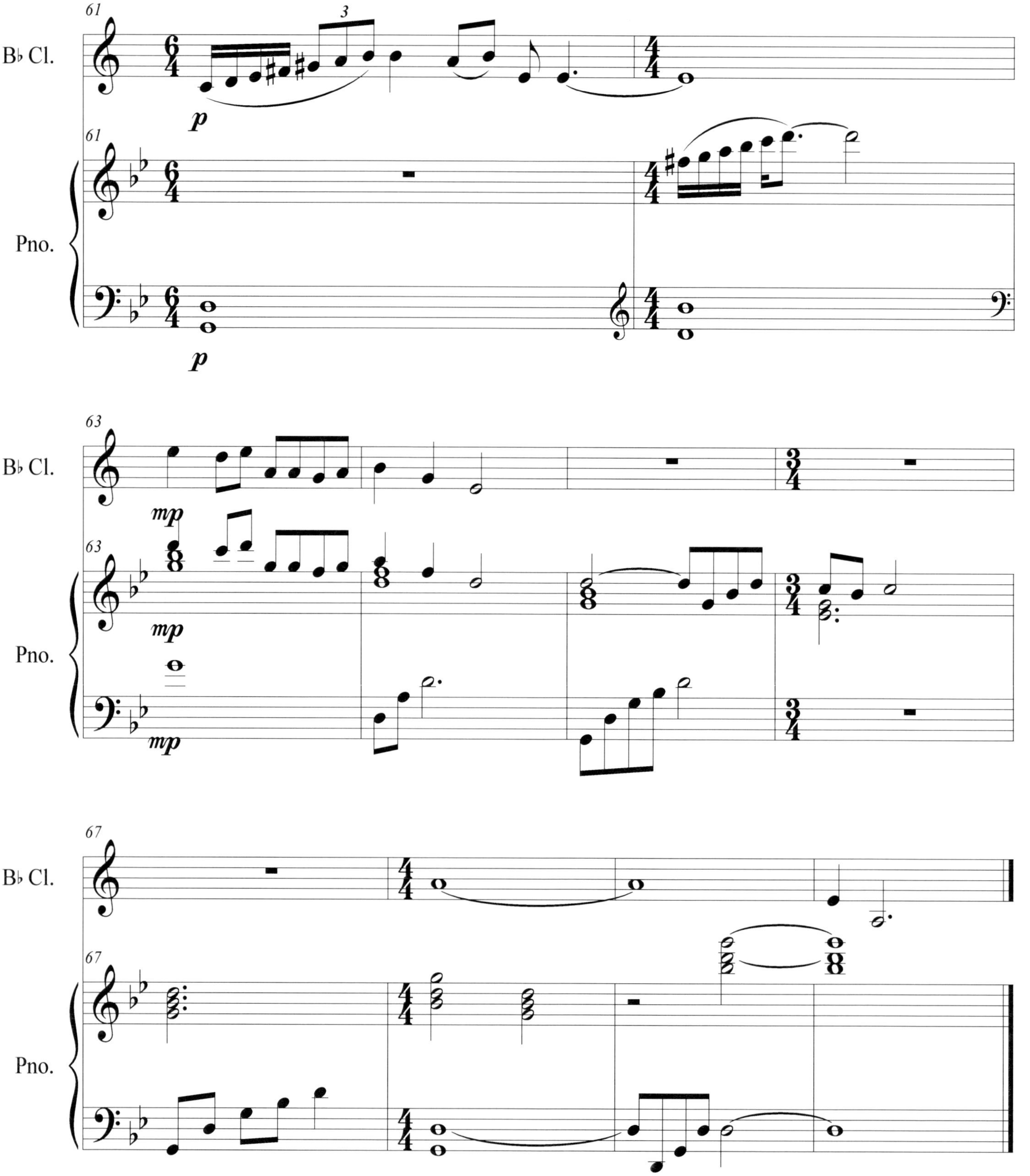
B♭ Cl.
Pno.
p
mp

*This page has been left blank to avoid an awkward page turn.*

# *Yorktown*

Colonial Fife and Drum Song

Arr. James Marshall

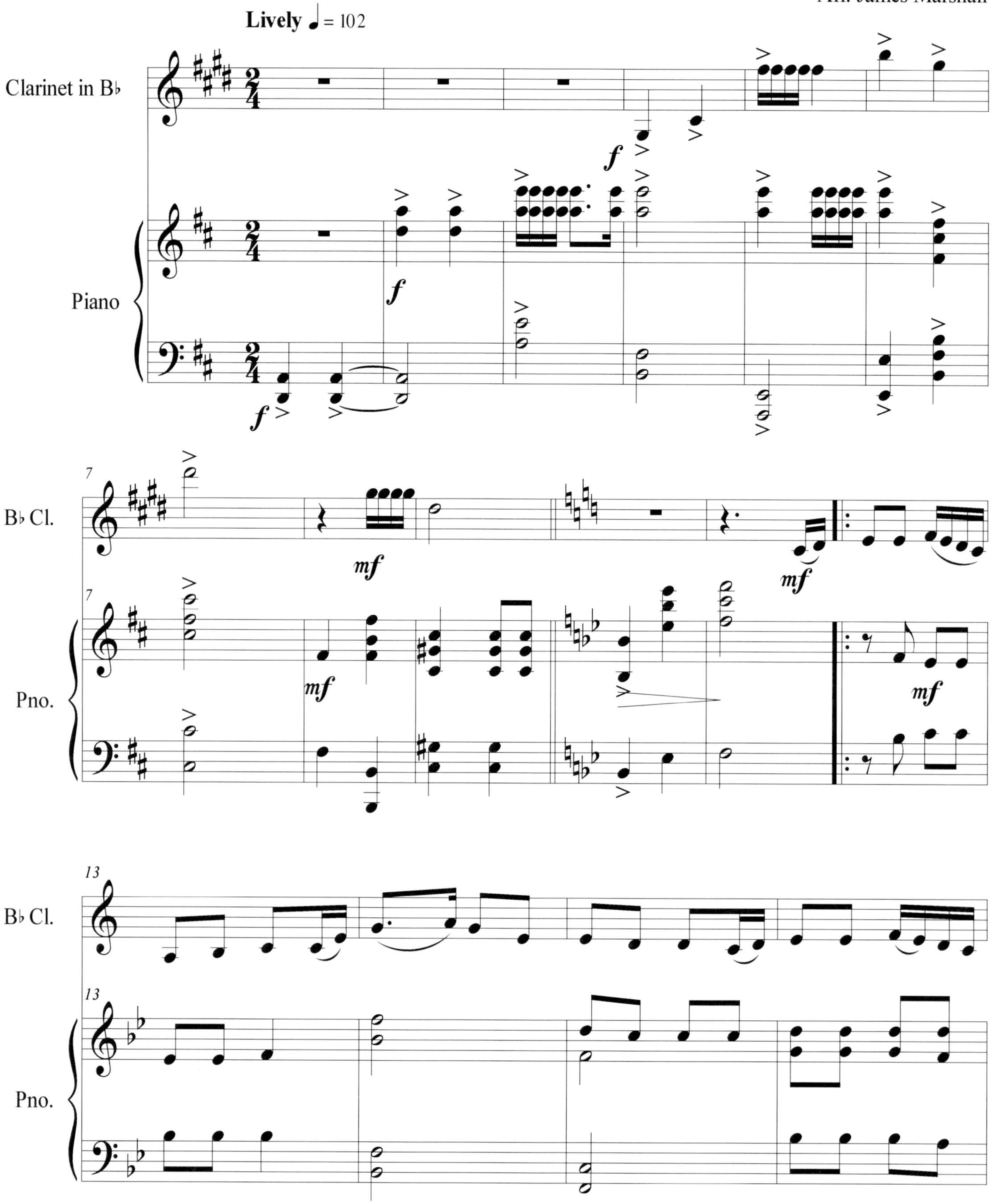

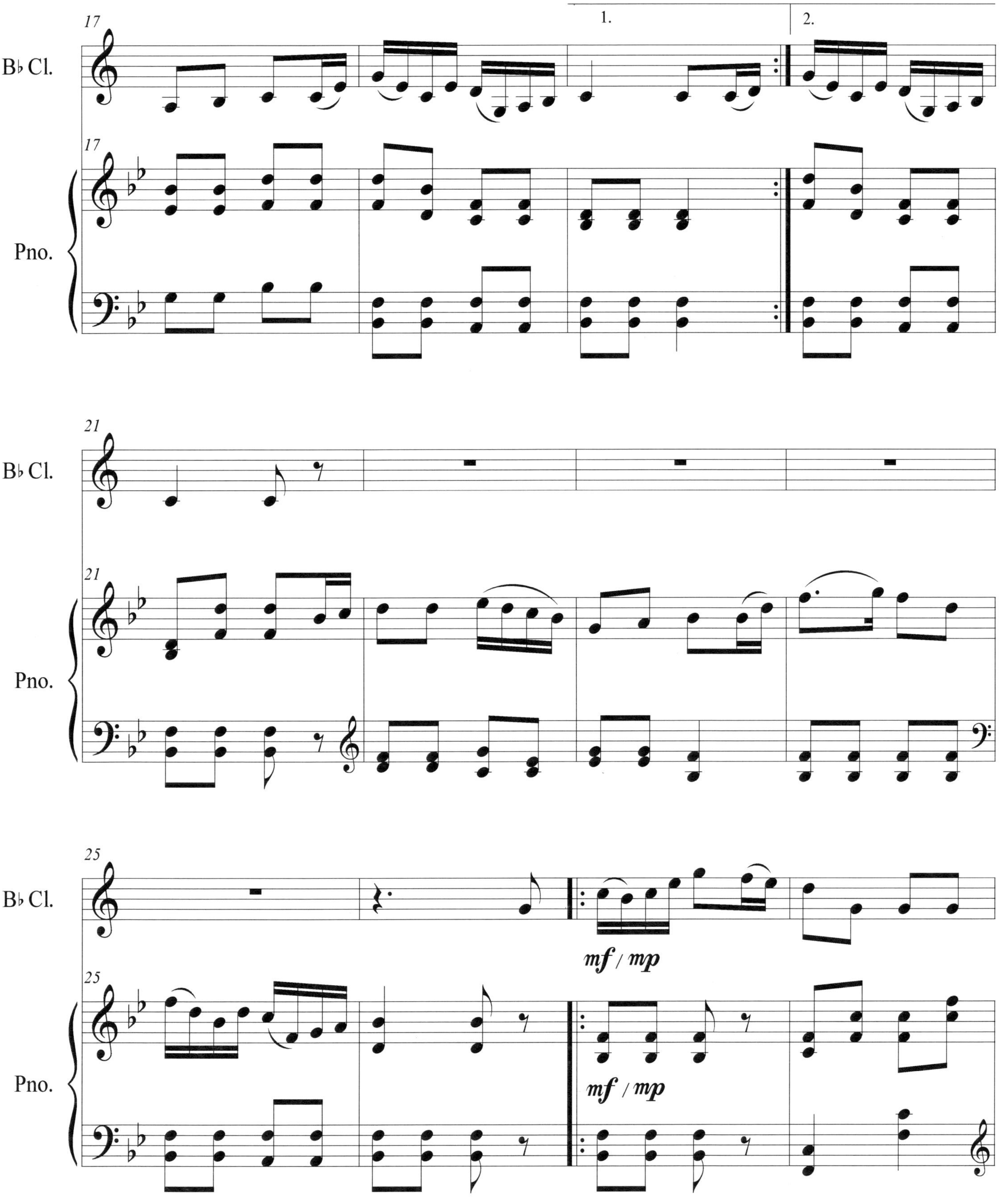
17
B♭ Cl.
Pno.
1.
2.
21
25
mf / mp

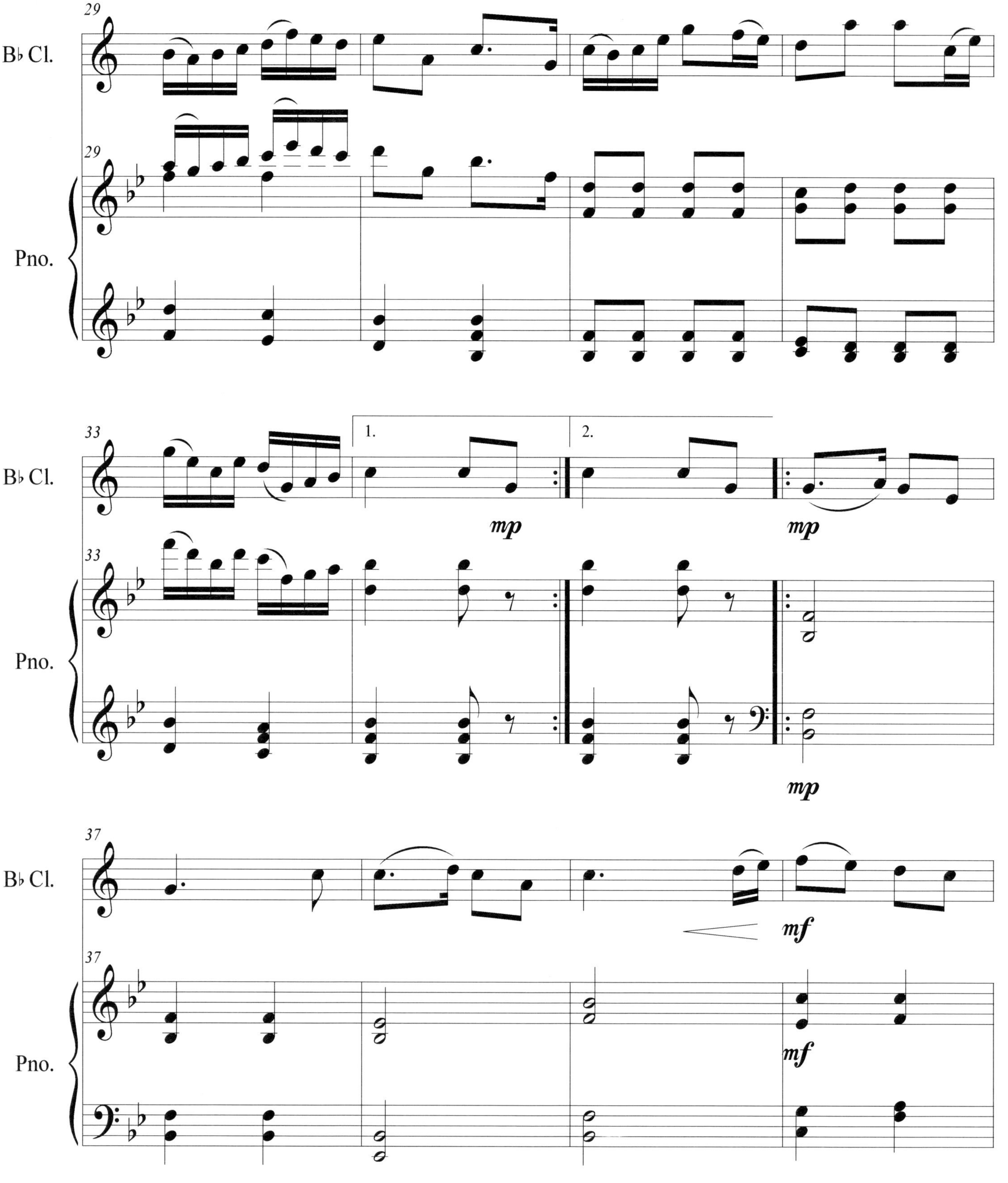
29
B♭ Cl.
29
Pno.
33
B♭ Cl.
1.
2.
mp
mp
33
Pno.
mp
37
B♭ Cl.
mf
37
Pno.
mf

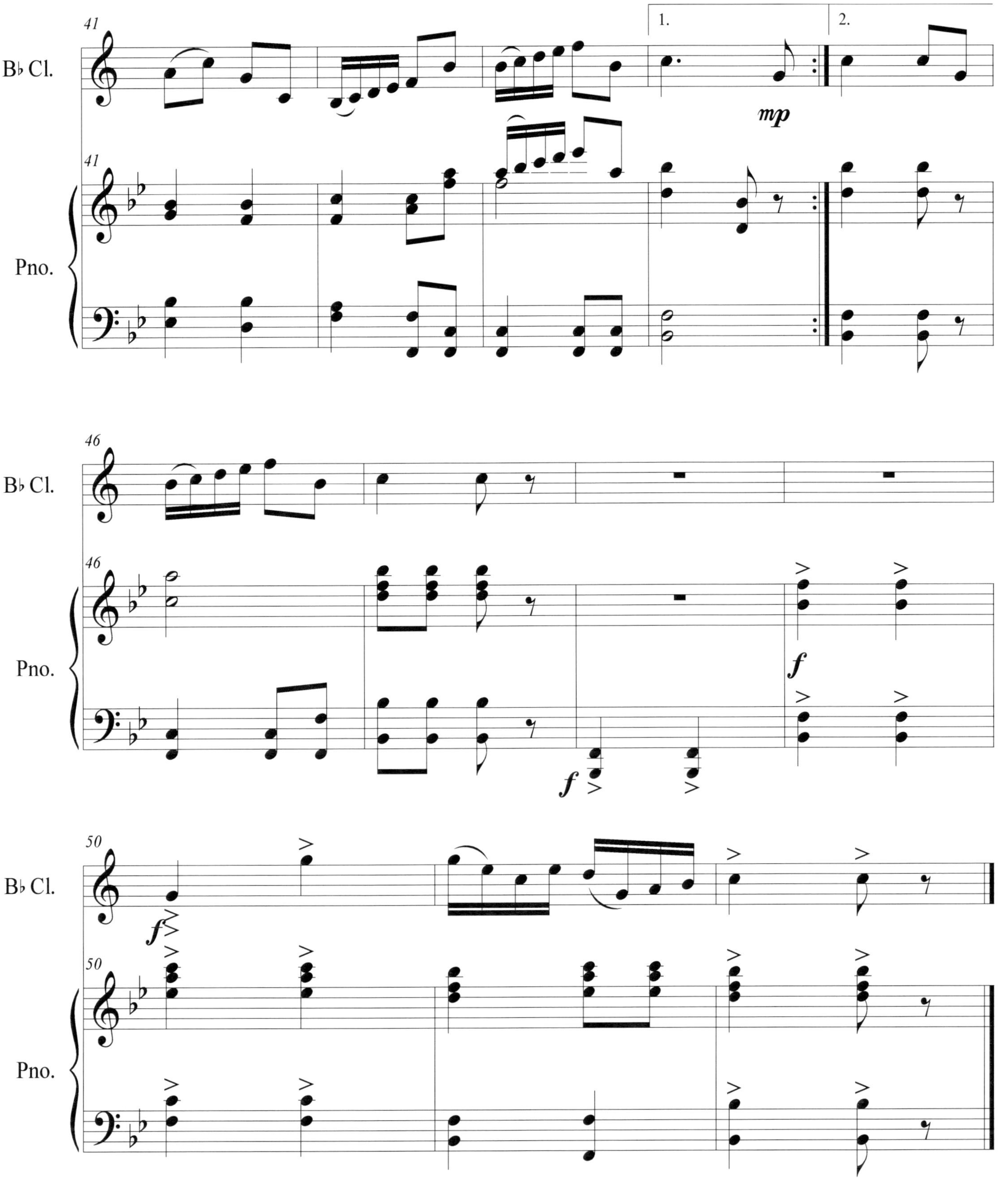
41
B♭ Cl.
Pno.
1.
2.
mp
46
f
50

# *Prospect*

Sacred Harp

Arr. James Marshall

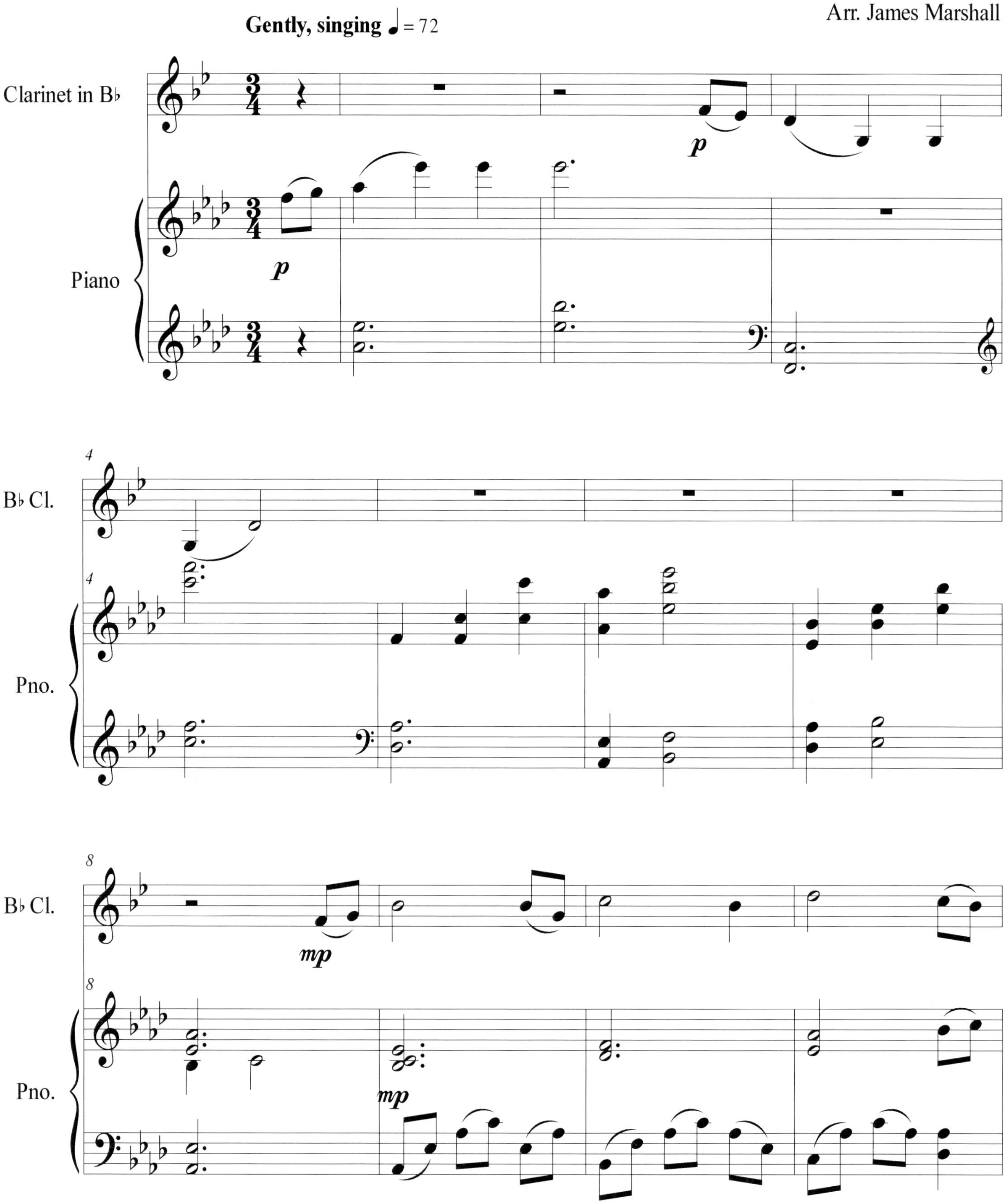

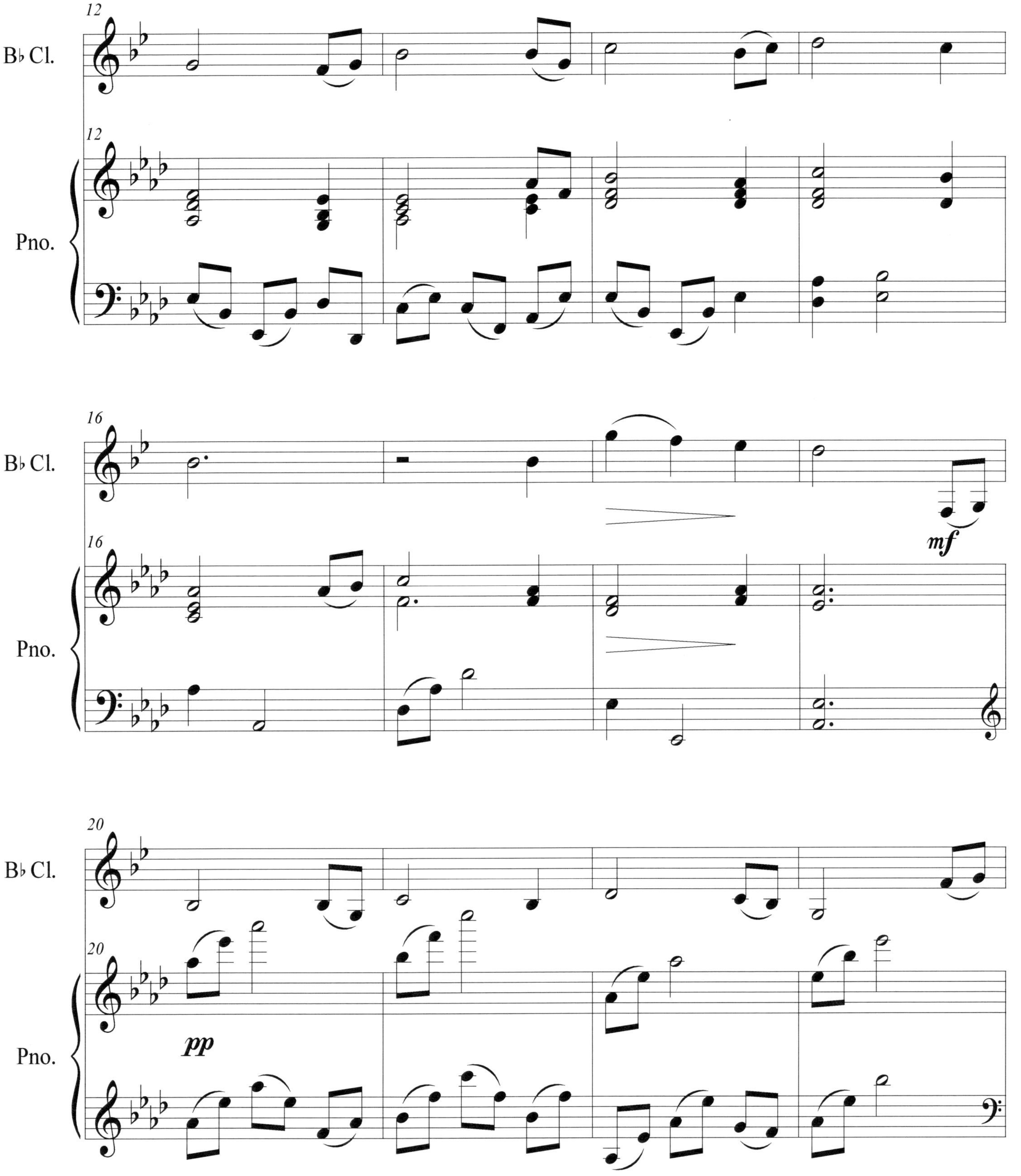
12
B♭ Cl.
12
Pno.
16
B♭ Cl.
16
mf
Pno.
20
B♭ Cl.
20
pp
Pno.

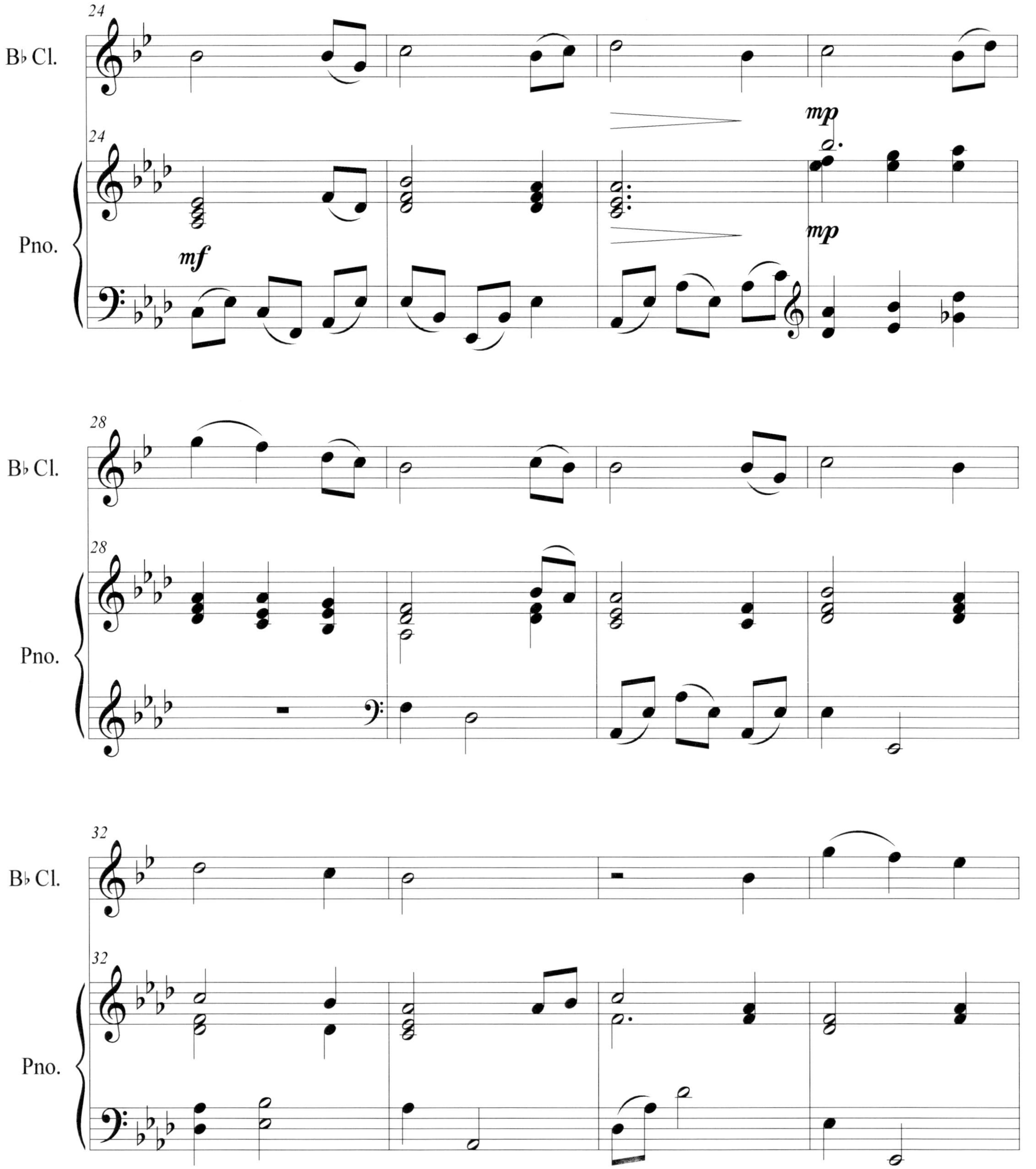
24
B♭ Cl.
24
Pno.
mf
mp
mp
28
B♭ Cl.
28
Pno.
32
B♭ Cl.
32
Pno.

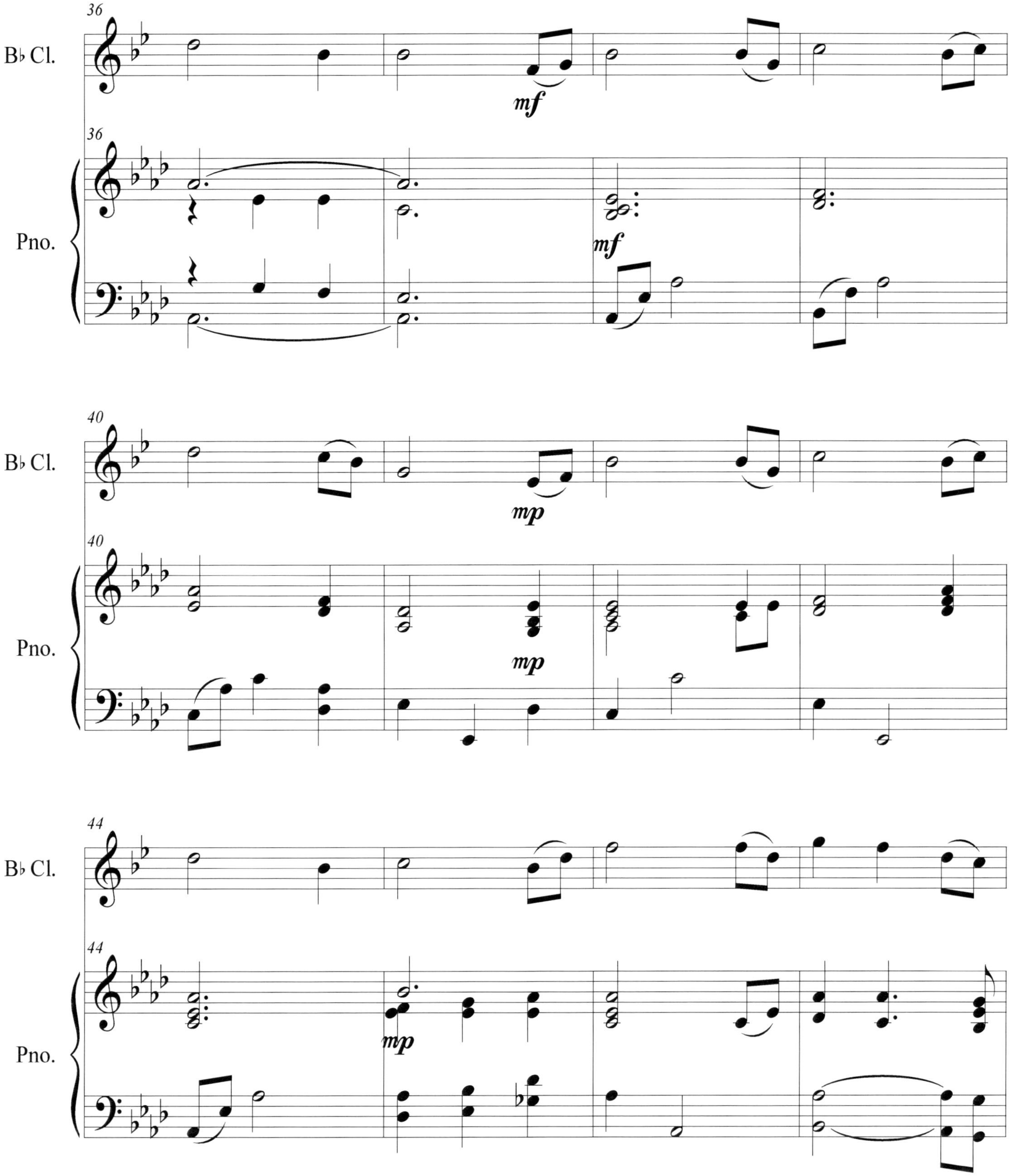
36
B♭ Cl.
mf
36
Pno.
mf
40
B♭ Cl.
mp
40
Pno.
mp
44
B♭ Cl.
44
Pno.
mp

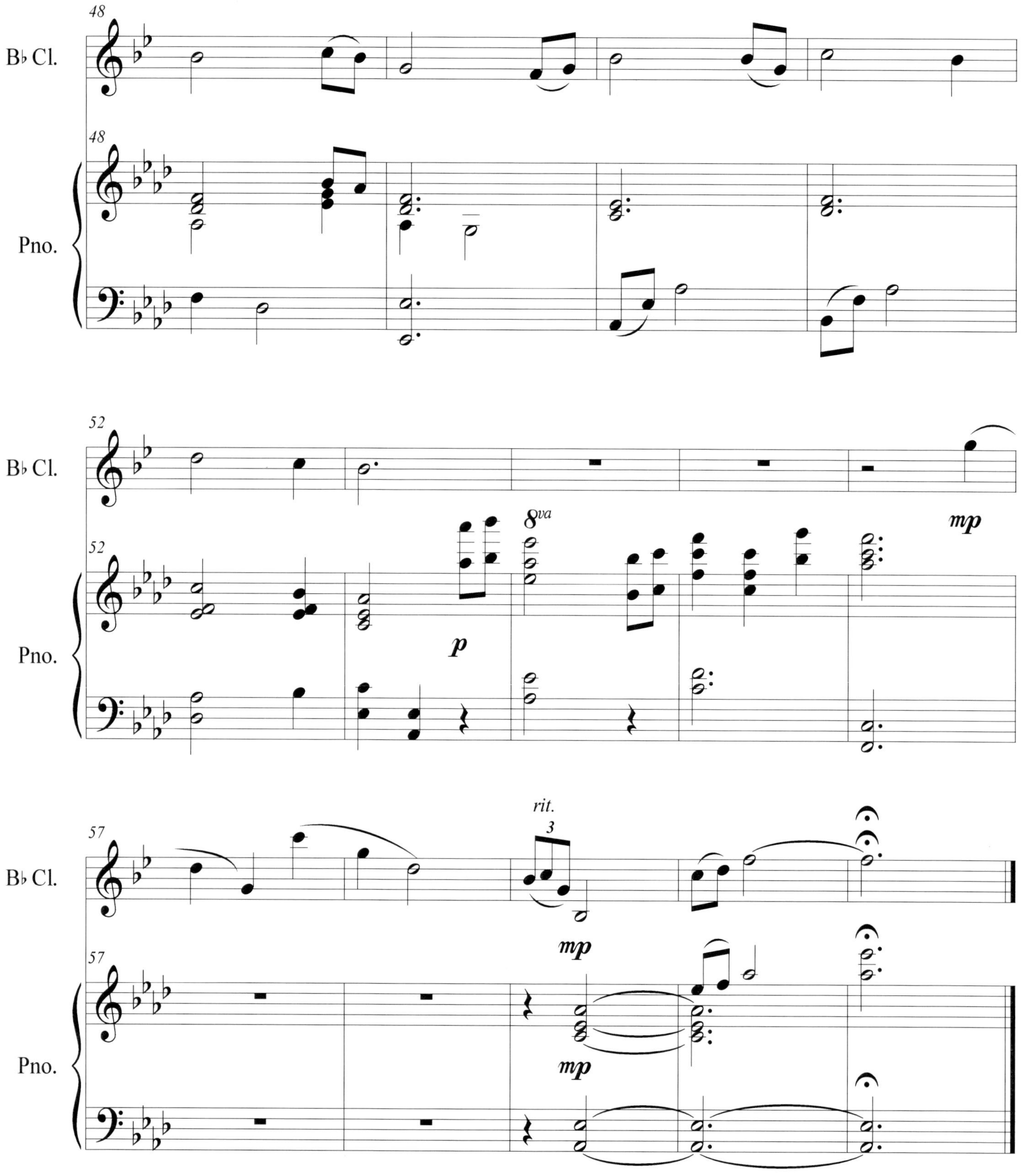
B♭ Cl.
Pno.
8va
p
mp
rit.

American Song Collection for

# Clarinet and Piano

James Marshall

Clarinet Solo Part

© 2021 by Mel Bay Publications, Inc. All Rights Reserved.

WWW.MELBAY.COM

# Preface

***American Song Collection for Clarinet and Piano*** is a set of ten songs primarily derived from the Colonial to Civil War eras. Moderate in difficulty for the clarinet with D above the staff as the highest note, these songs find a unique expression in the hauntingly lyrical tone of the instrument. The wide ranges of both the piano and clarinet offer further textural pairings and contrasts within a traditional chordal harmonic framework with colorations of fourths, fifths, and occasional added tones. The collection consists of ballads, traditional and sacred songs including tunes from the "Sacred Harp" shape-note tradition. The most adventurous and colorful arrangement, "Black Is the Color of My True Love's Hair" shows more recent influences of Gershwin, Debussy, and Southern jazz.

"Prospect", the final song from the "Sacred Harp", includes the lyric:

*Oh if my Lord would come to meet*
*my soul would strength her wings in haste*
*Fly fearless through Death's iron gate*
*Nor feel the terrors as she passed.*

My thanks to William Bay for his guidance and advice in the creation of this collection.

**Song Listing**:

*Morning Song* – "Sacred Harp"
*Amazing Grace* – Music from "Virginia Harmony", Lyrics by John Newton
*Hard Times, Come Again* – Stephen Foster
*Camptown Races* – Reel – Stephen Foster
*Anthem* – "Sacred Harp"
*Black Is the Color of My True Love's Hair* – Southern Appalachian Folk Song
*Aura Lee* – Civil War Song
*Poor Wayfaring Stranger* – American Folk Song
*Yorktown* – Colonial Fife and Drum Song
*Prospect* – "Sacred Harp"

*James Marshall*

# *Index of Solos*

# *Morning Song*

Clarinet in B♭

Kentucky Harmony
Arr. James Marshall

**Andante** ♩ = 80

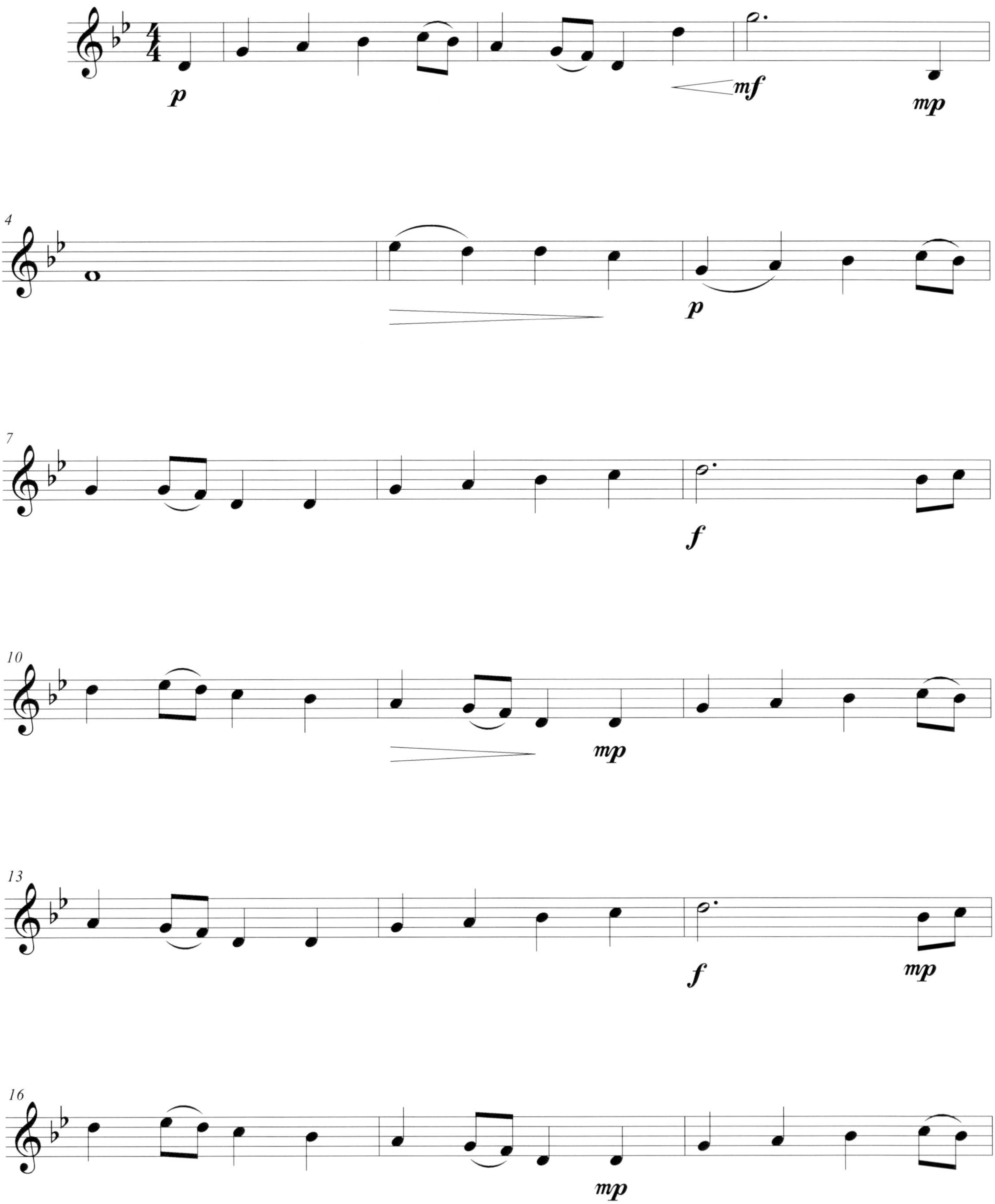

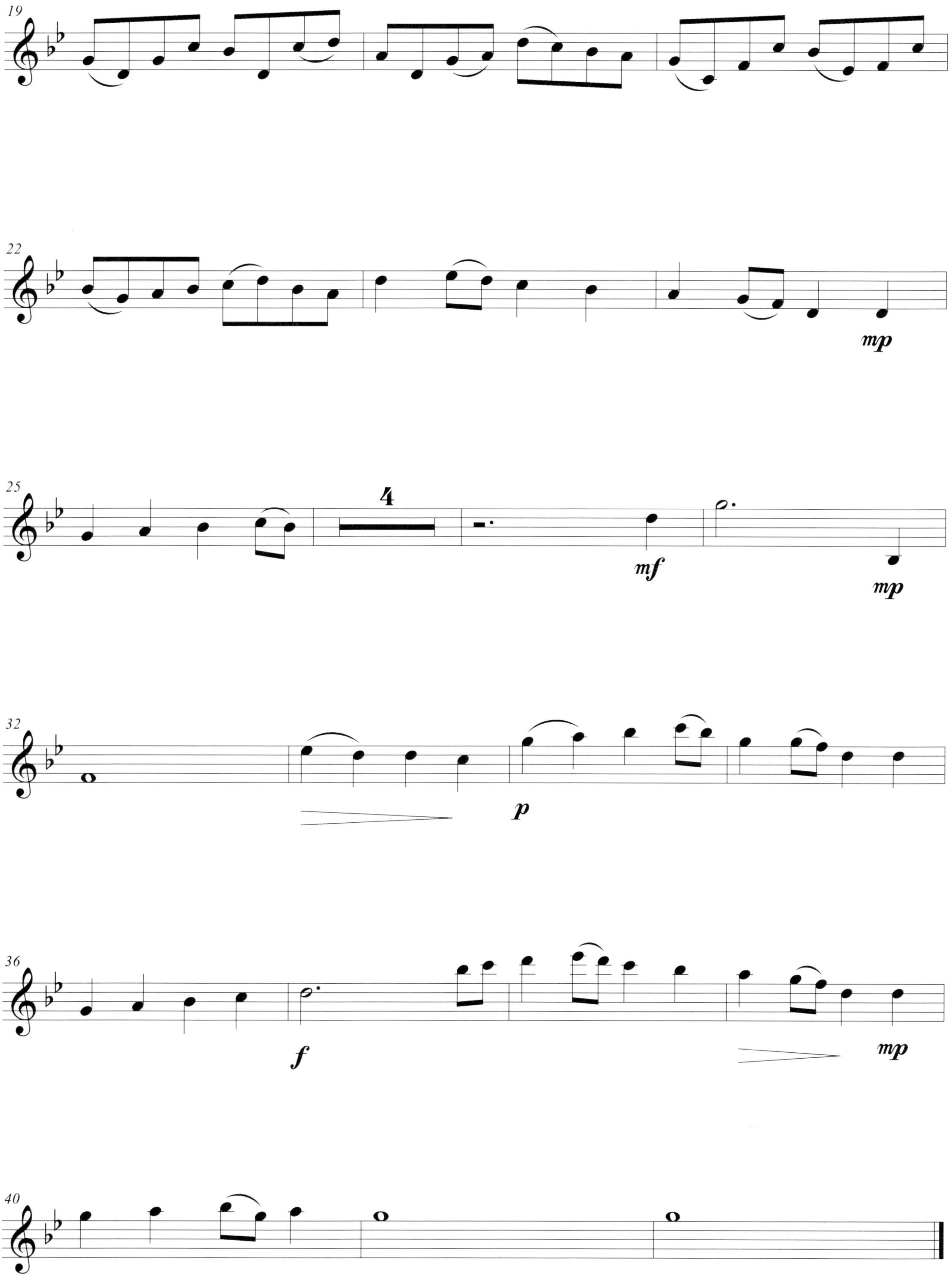
19
22
mp
25
4
mf
mp
32
p
36
f
mp
40

# *Amazing Grace*

Clarinet in B♭

Early American Melody

Arr. James Marshall

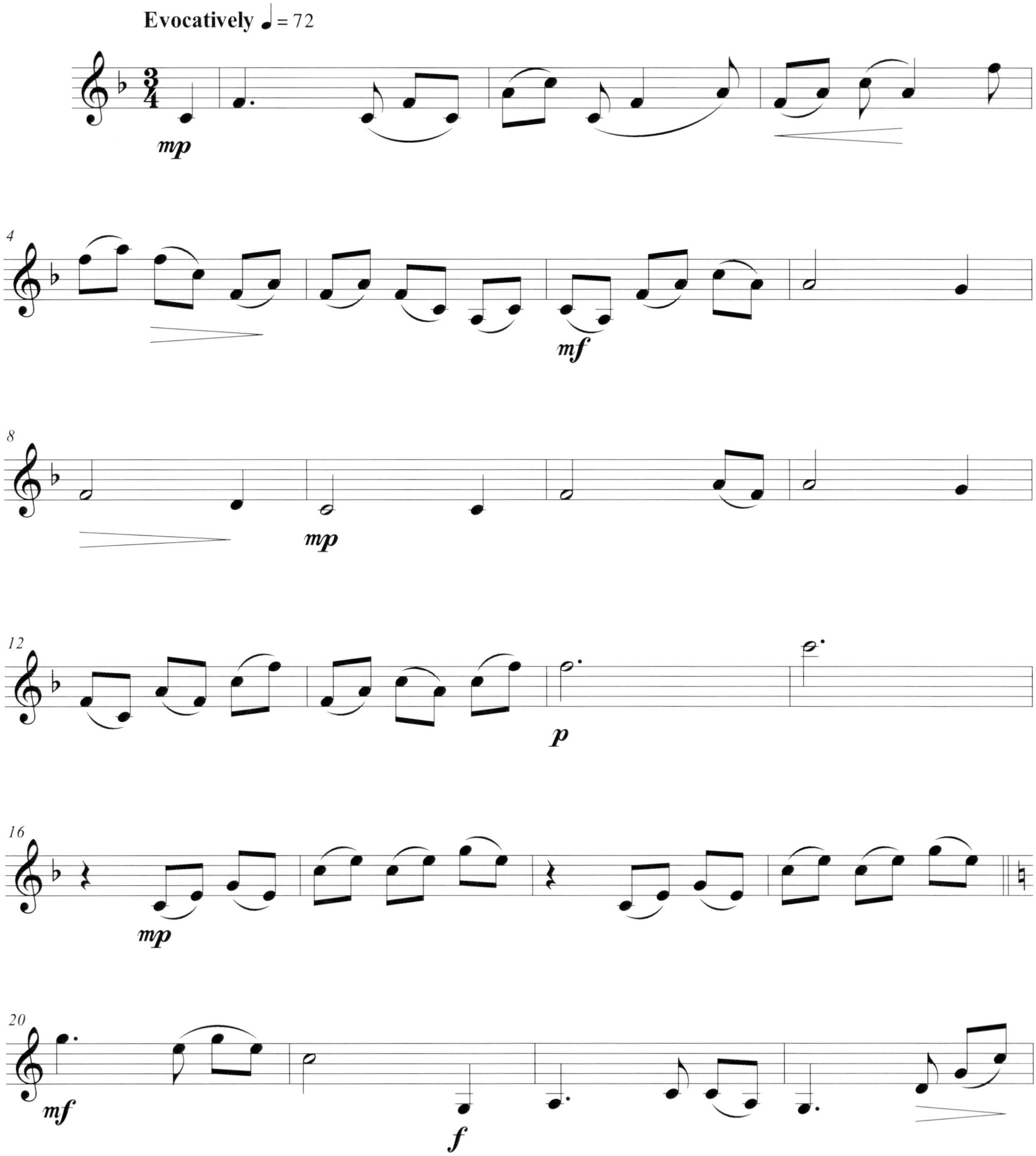

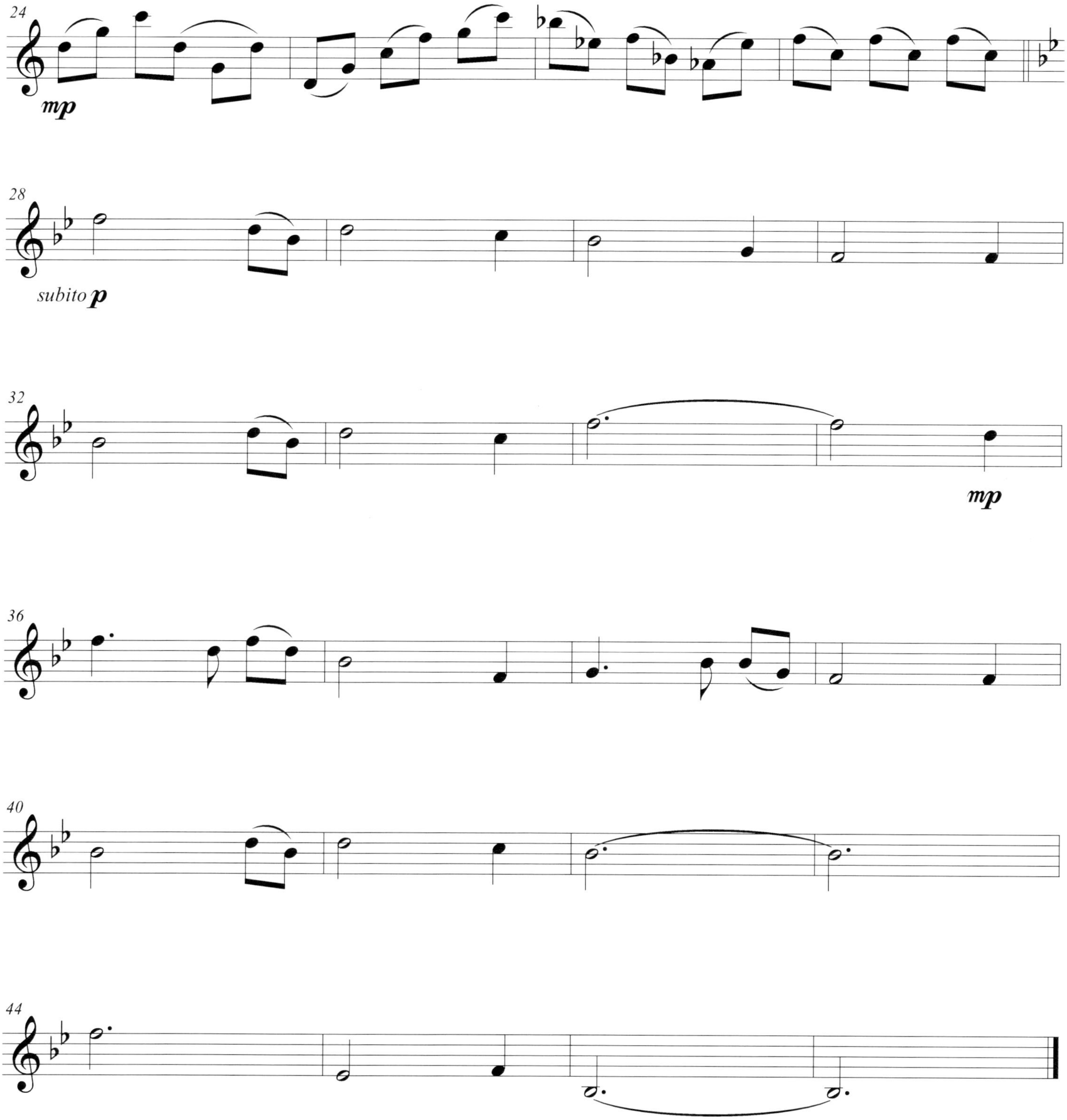
24
mp
28
subito p
32
mp
36
40
44

# *Hard Times, Come Again No More*

Clarinet in B♭

Stephen Foster
Arr. James Marshall

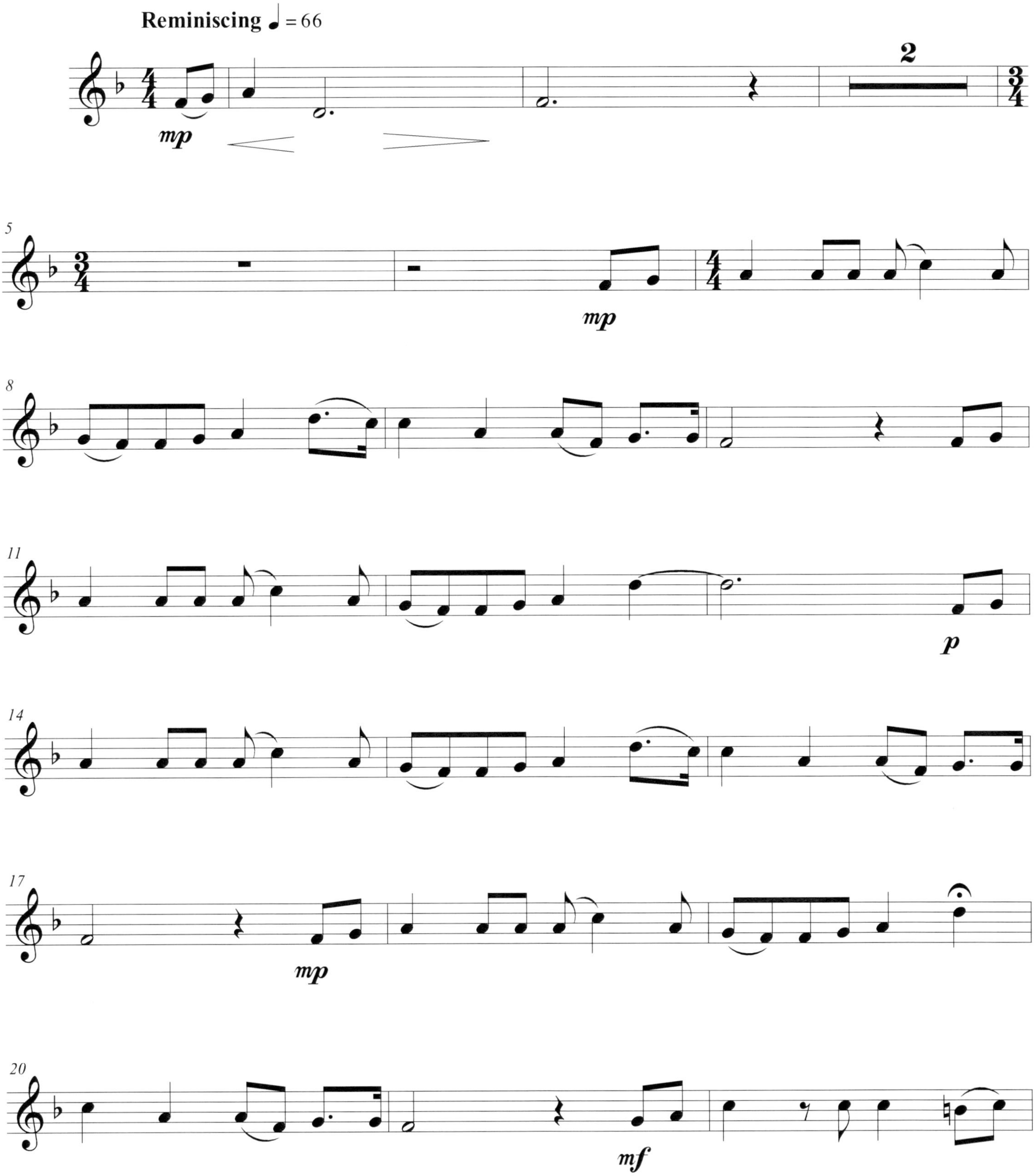

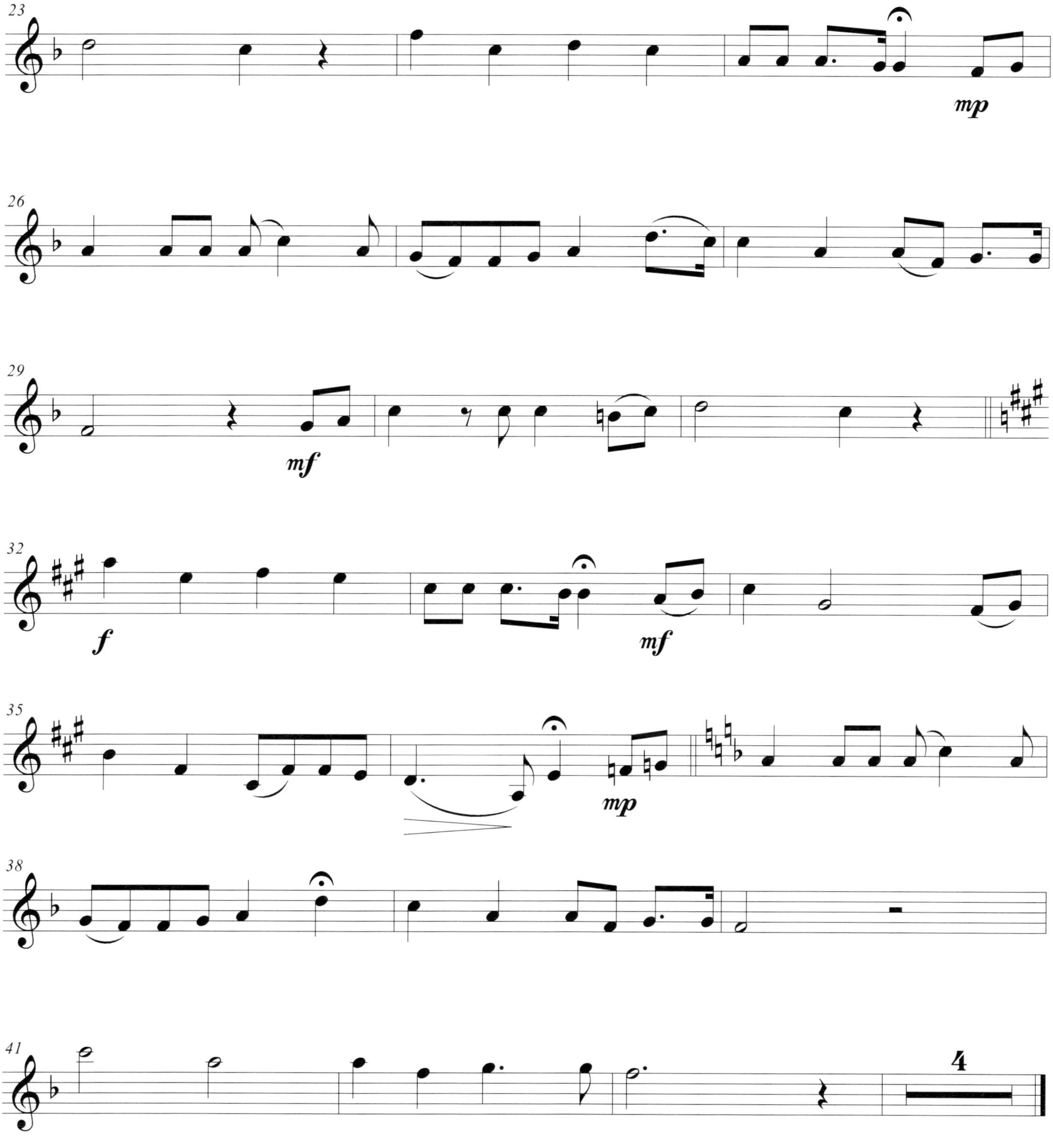
23
mp
26
29
mf
32
f
mf
35
mp
38
41
4

# *Camptown Races - Reel*

Clarinet in B♭

Stephen Foster

Arr. James Marshall

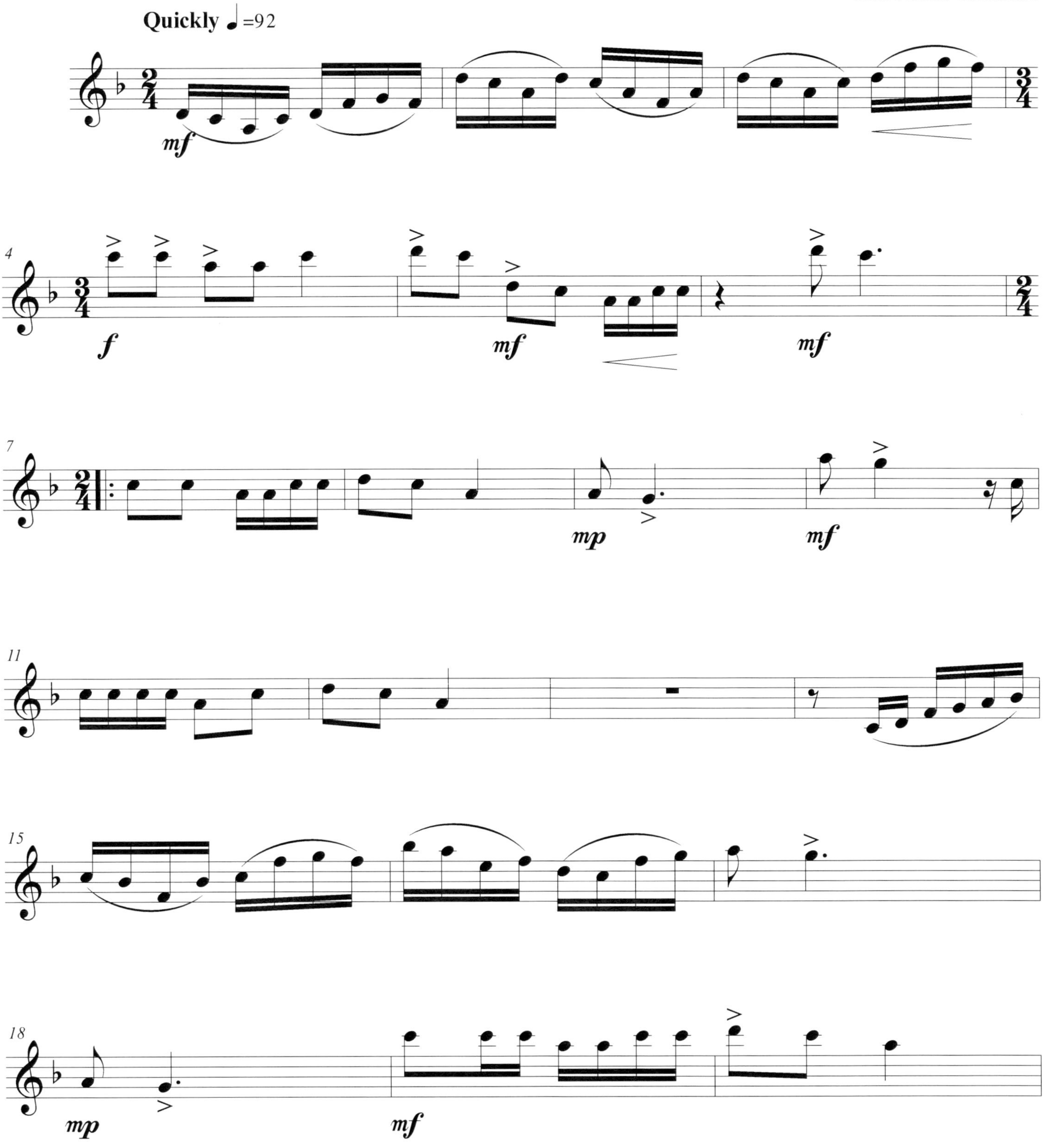

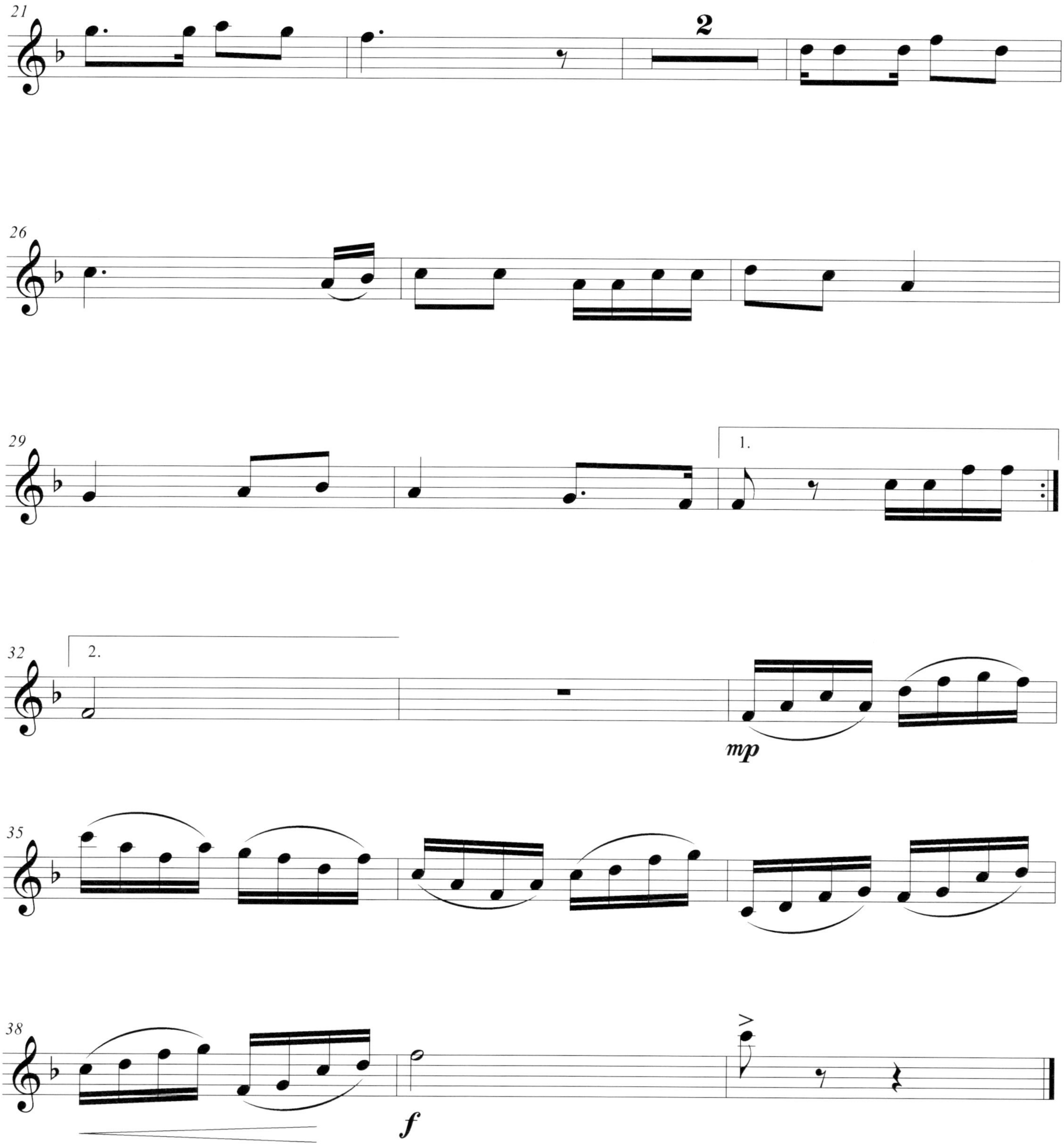
21
2
26
29
1.
32
2.
mp
35
38
f

# Anthem

Clarinet in B♭

Sacred Harp

Arr. James Marshall

**Uplifting, gently lilting** ♩ = 90

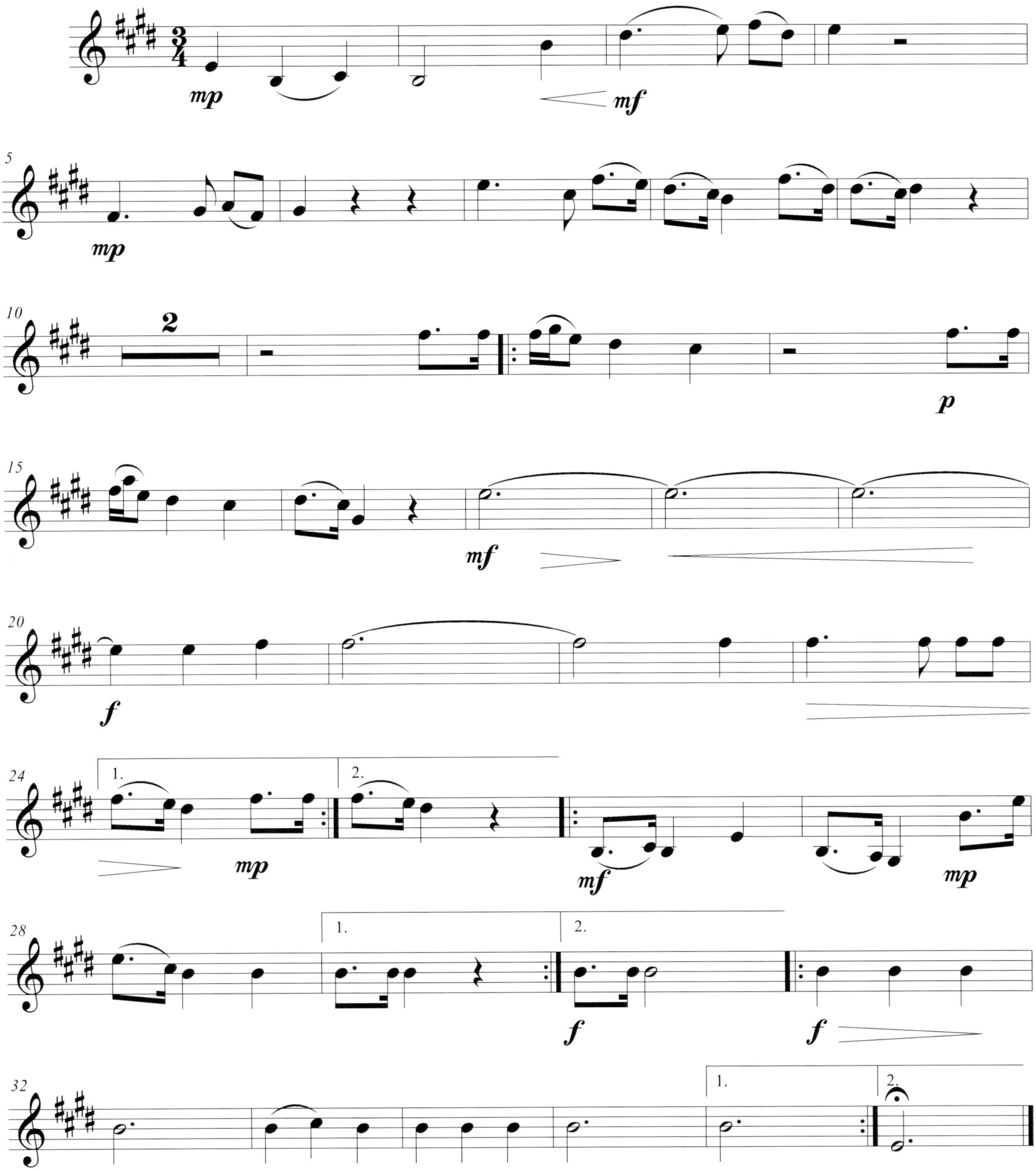

*This page has been left blank to avoid an awkward page turn.*

# *Poor Wayfaring Stranger*

American Folk Song
Arr. James Marshall

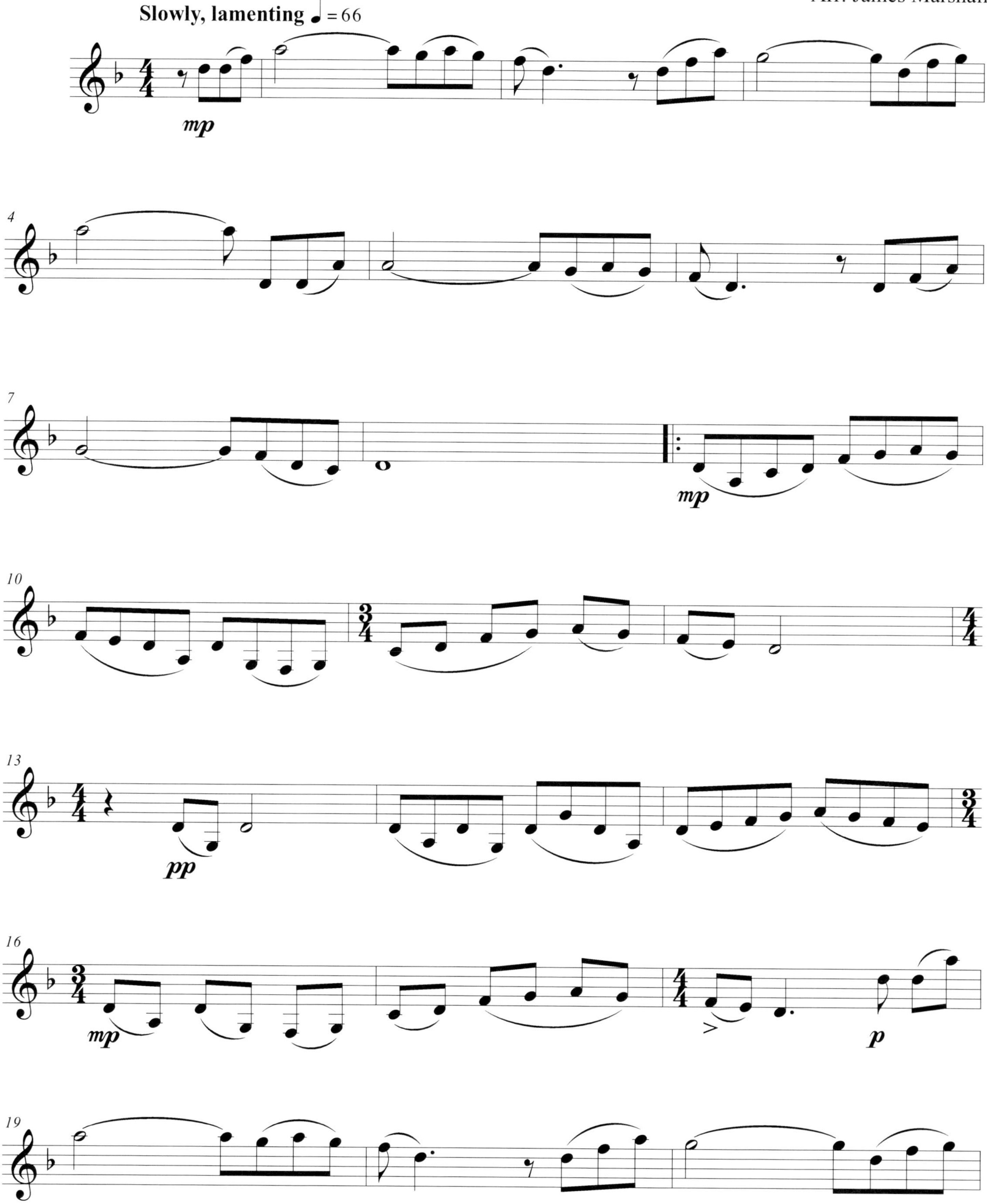

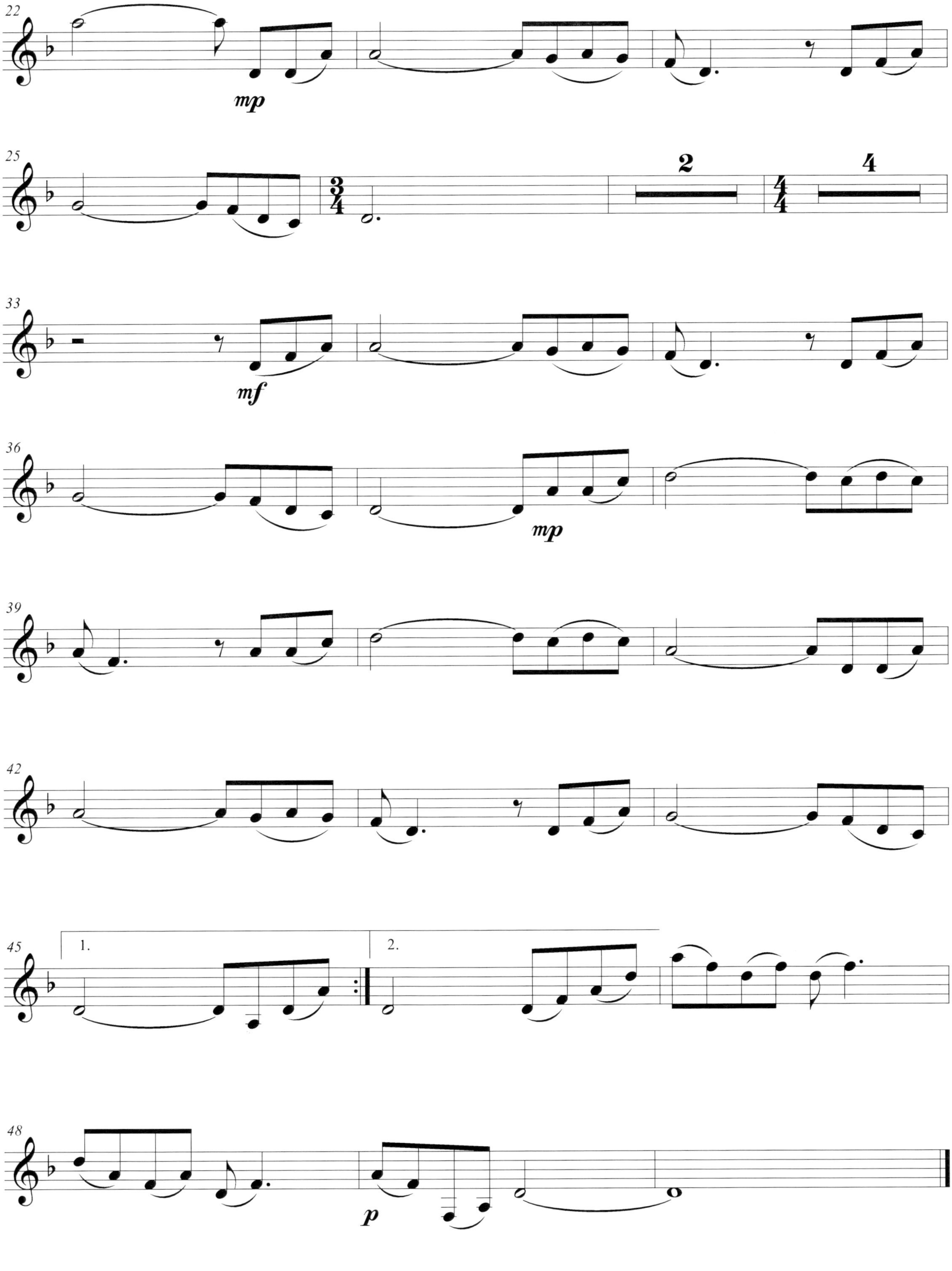
22
mp
25
2
4
33
mf
36
mp
39
42
45
1.
2.
48
p

# *Aura Lee*

Clarinet in B♭

Civil War Song

Arr. James Marshall

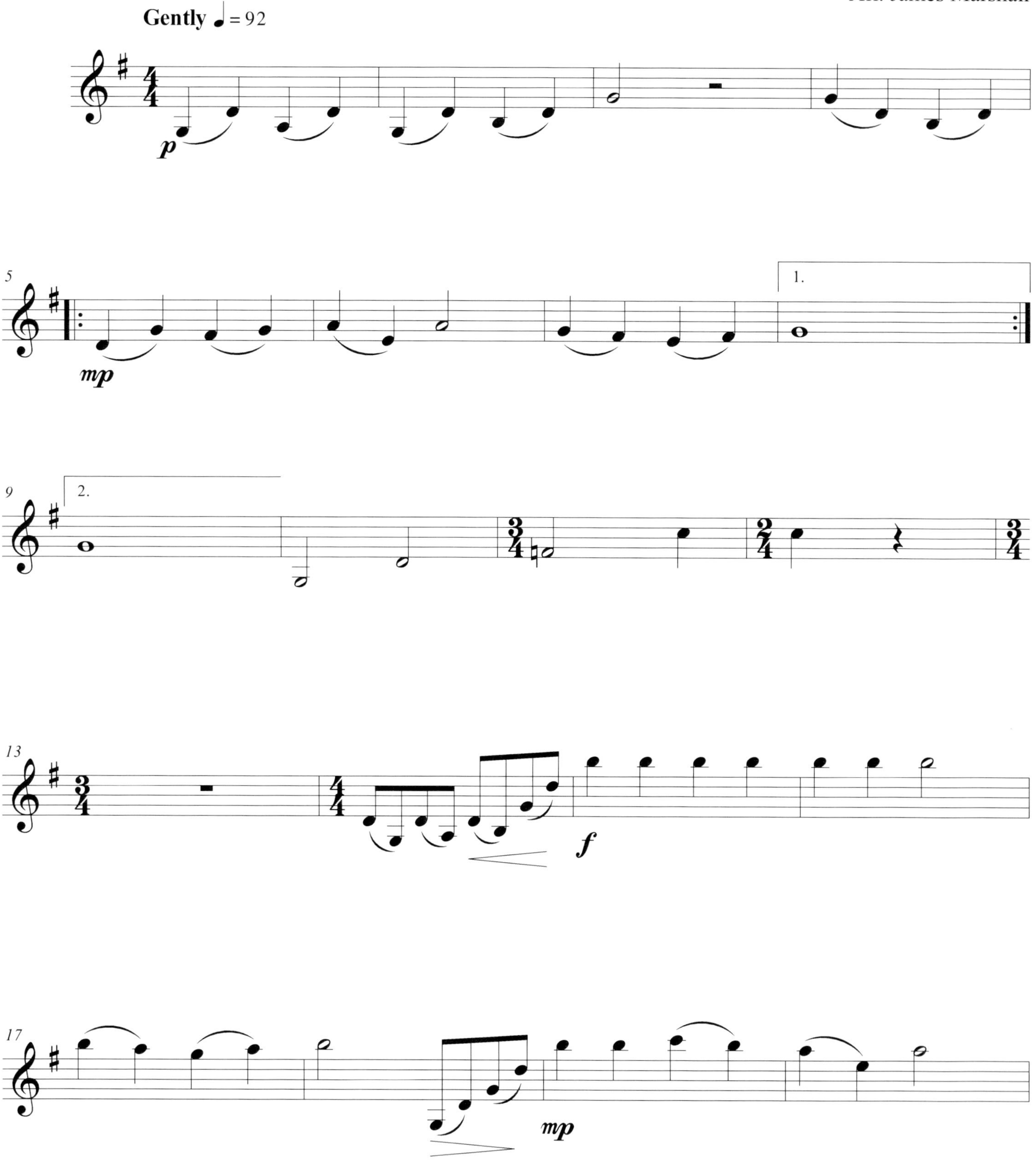

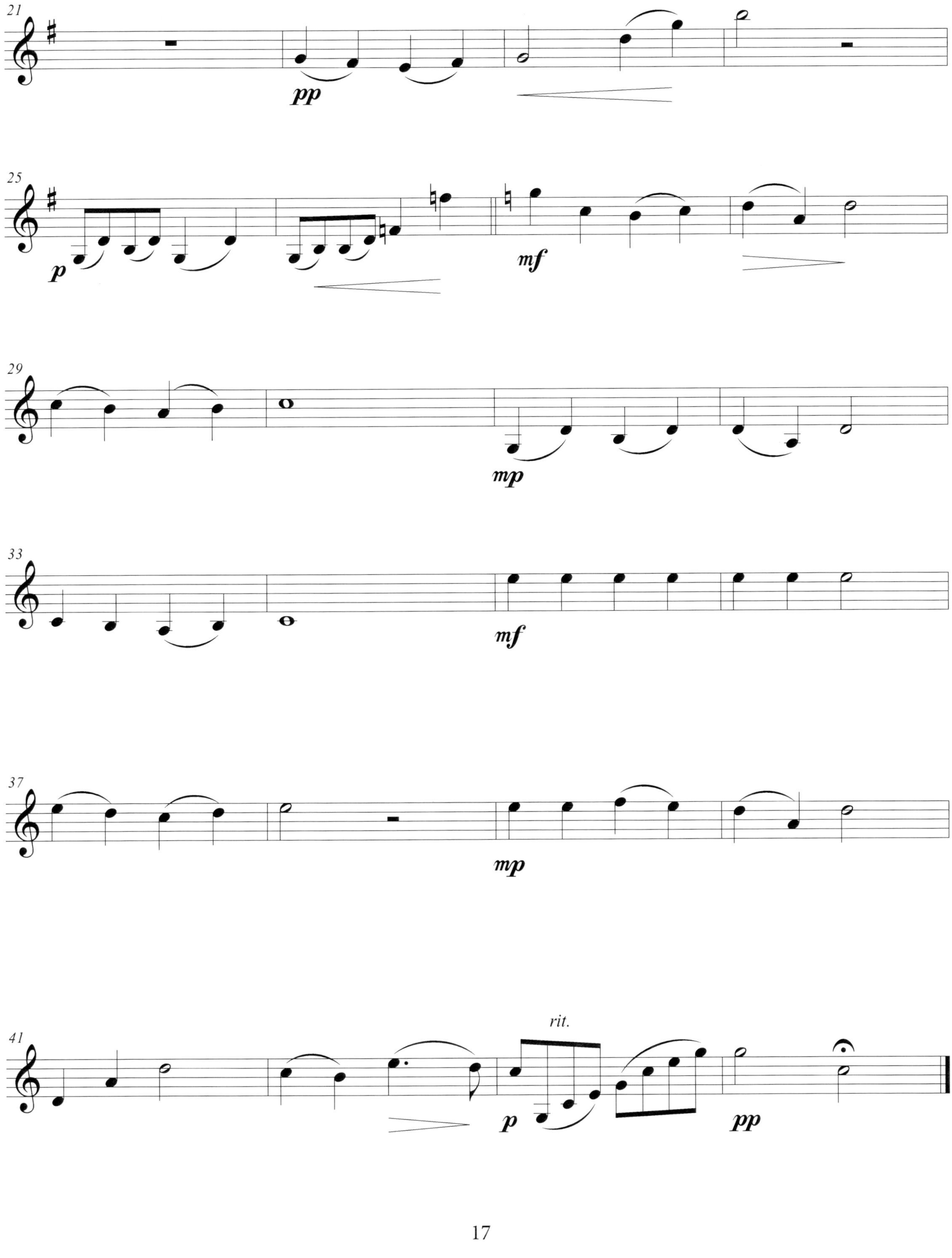
21
pp
25
p
mf
29
mp
33
mf
37
mp
41
rit.
p
pp

# *Yorktown*

Clarinet in B♭

Colonial Fife and Drum Song

Arr. James Marshall

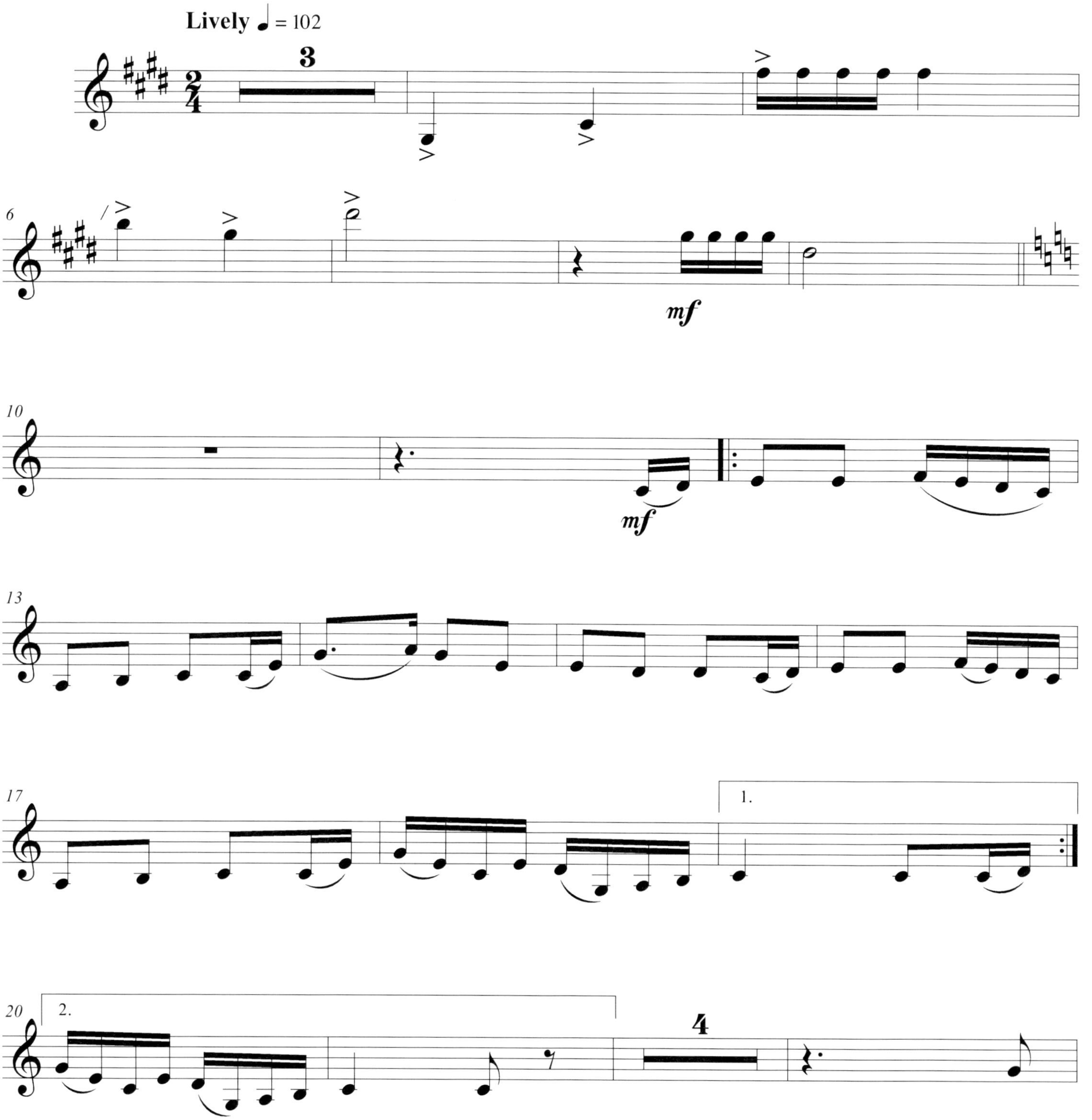

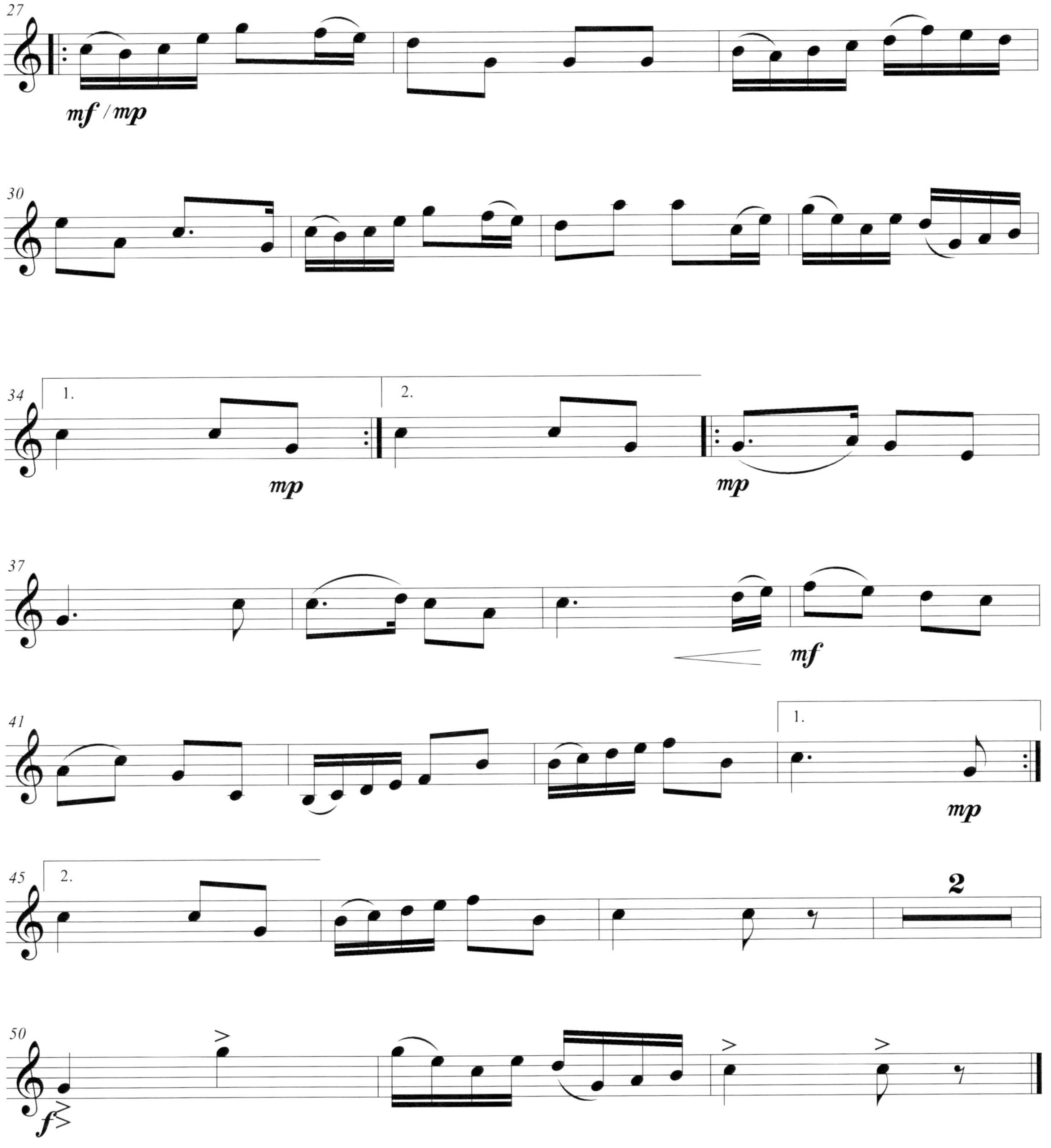
mf / mp
1.
2.
mp
mp
mf
1.
mp
2.
2
f

# *Prospect*

Clarinet in B♭

Sacred Harp

Arr. James Marshall

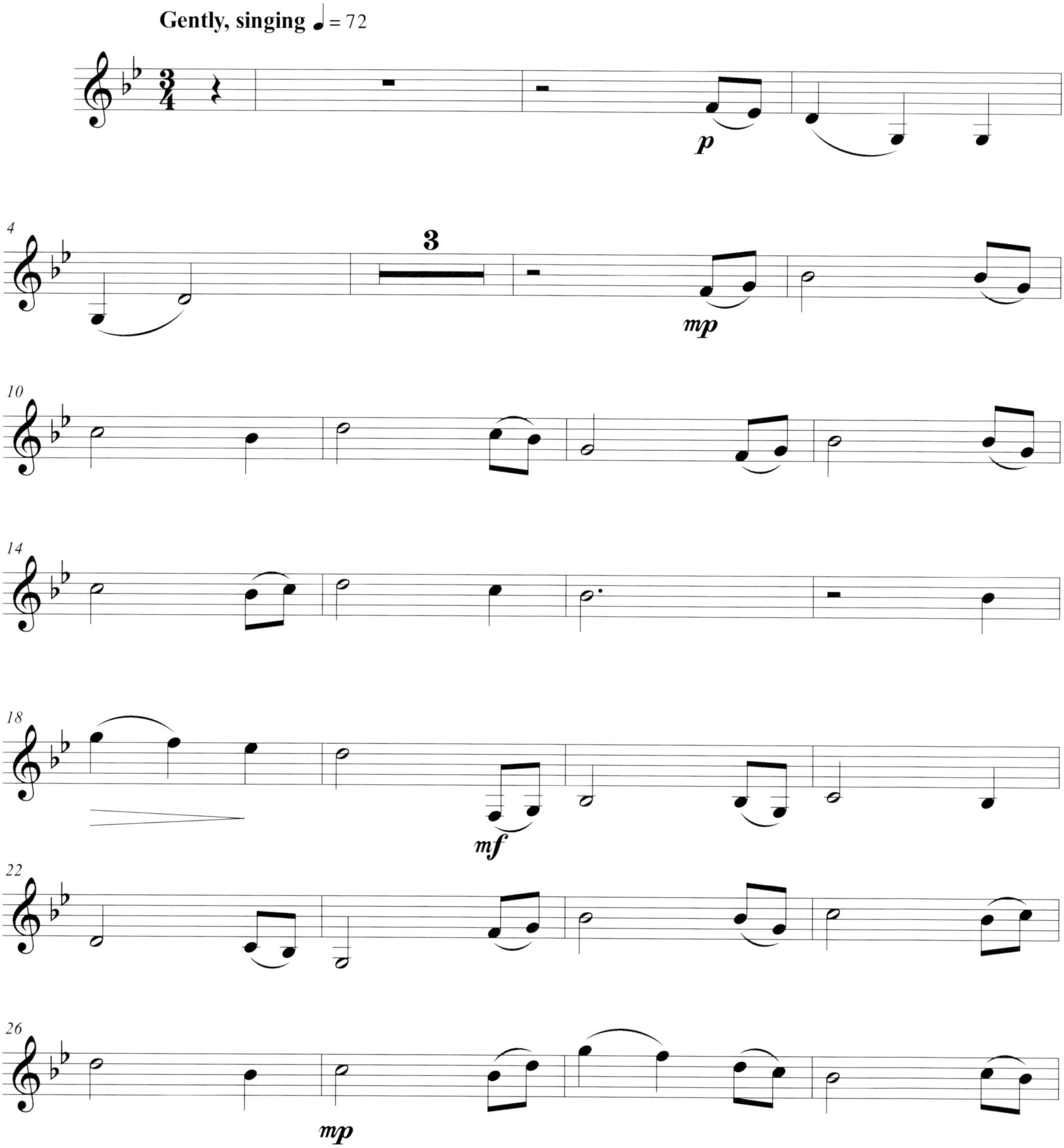

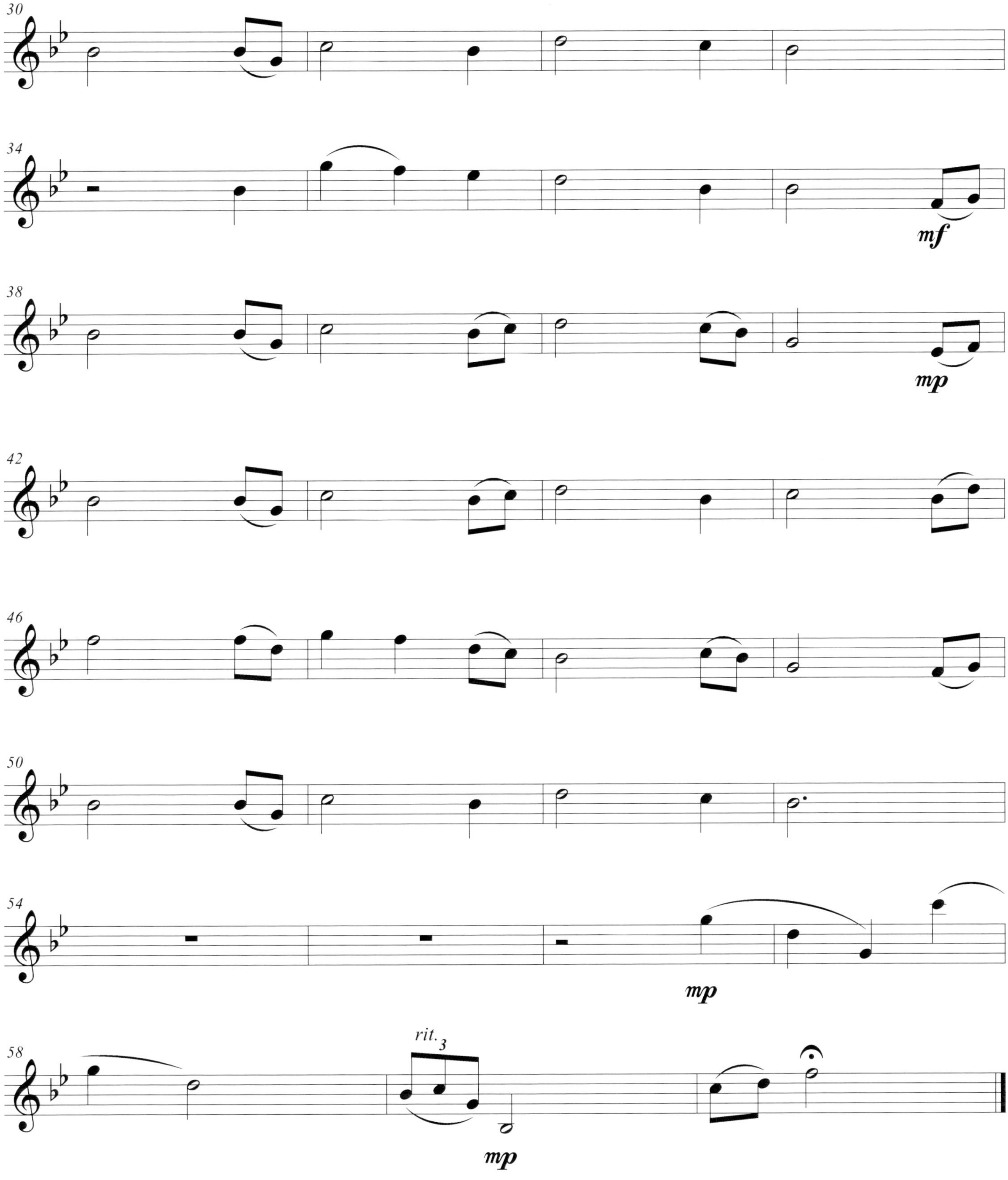
30
34
mf
38
mp
42
46
50
54
mp
58
rit.
3
mp

# Black Is the Color of My True Love's Hair

Clarinet in B♭

Southern Appalachian Folk Song

Arr. James Marshall

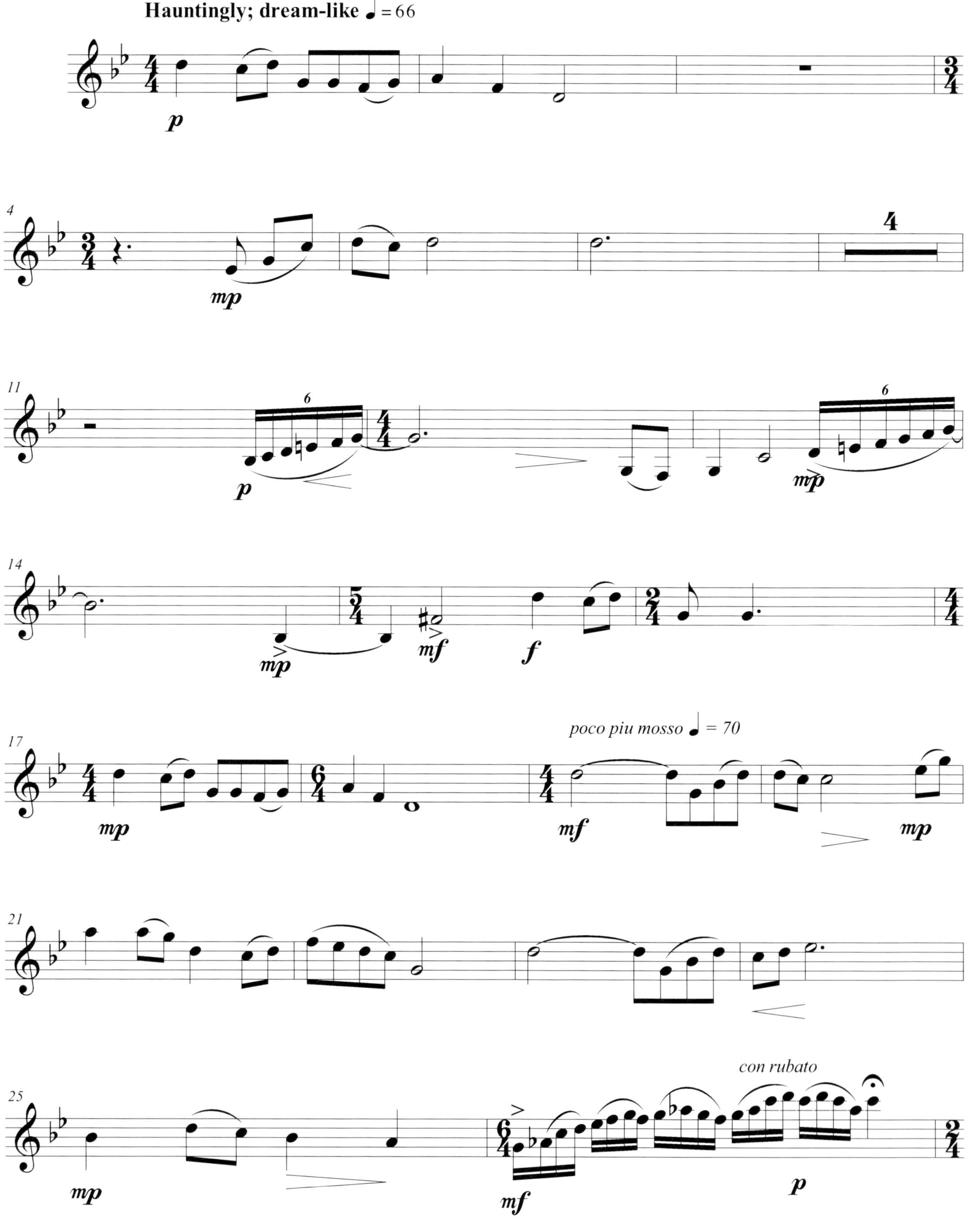

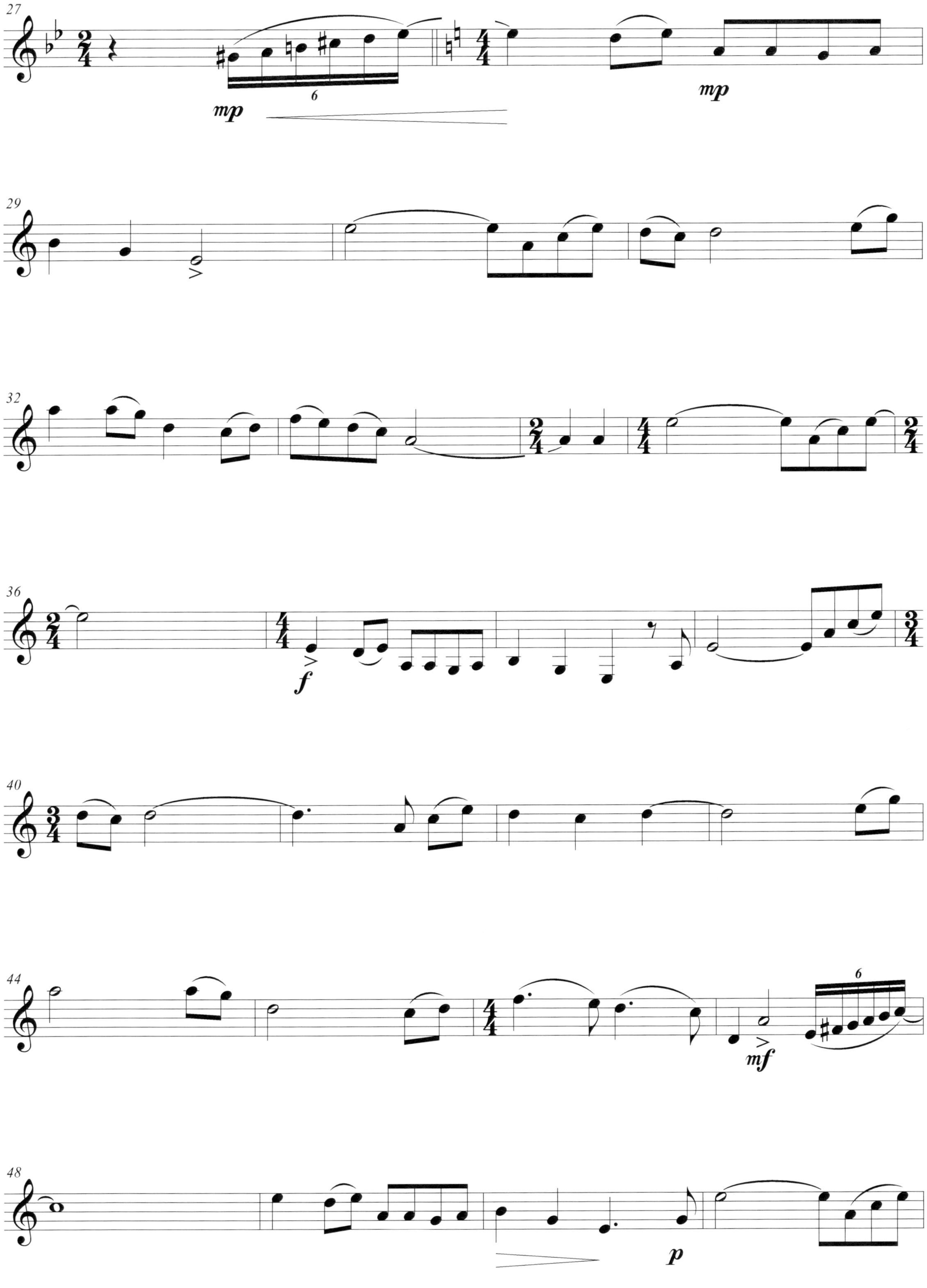
27
mp
6
mp
29
32
36
f
40
44
6
mf
48
p

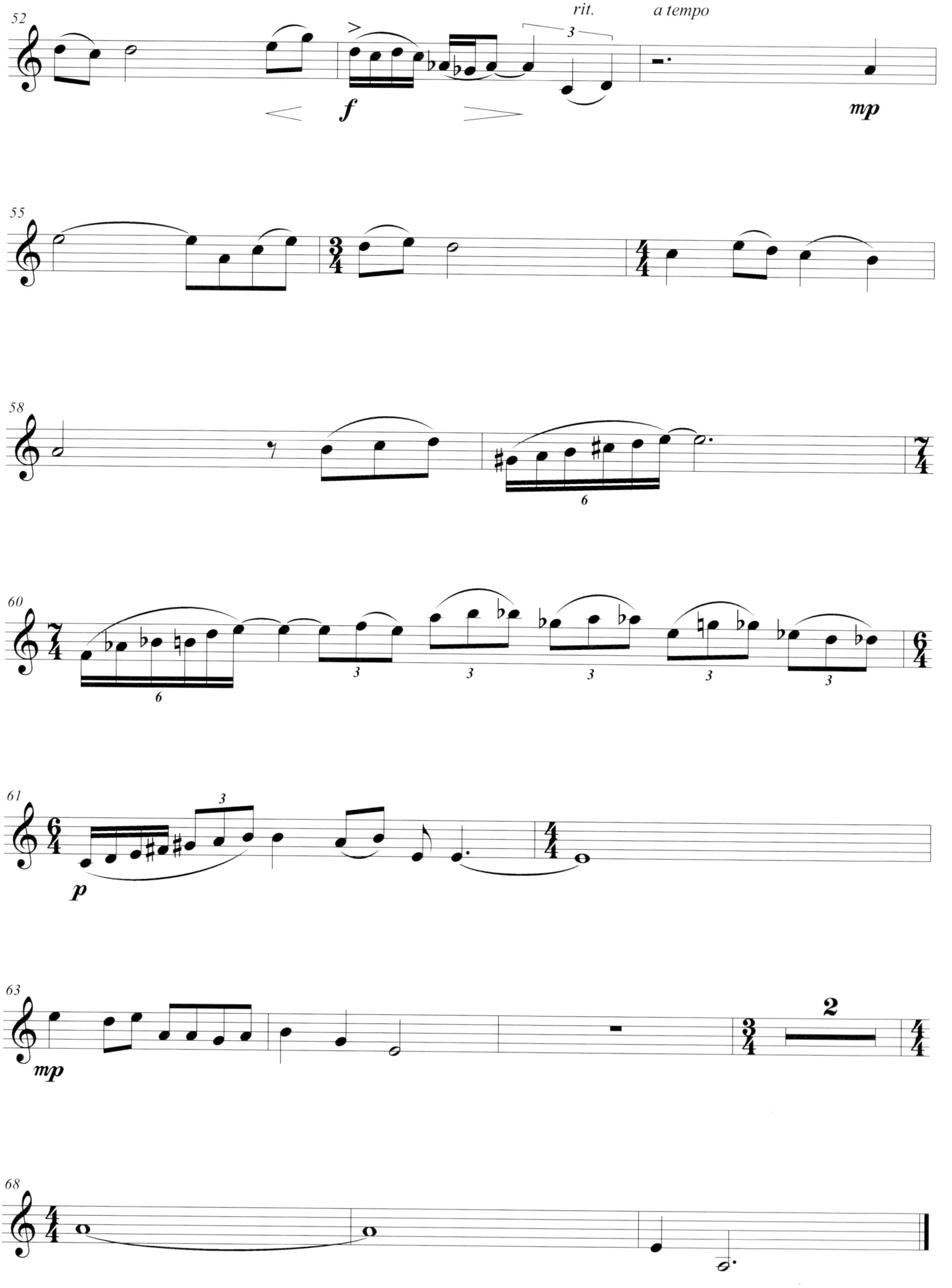
rit.
a tempo
mp
mp